Supernatural Superpowers

TREVOR DEARING

Edited by Howard Earl

LOGOS INTERNATIONAL
Plainfield, New Jersey

All Scripture taken from the Revised Standard Version of
the Holy Bible unless otherwise noted.

Supernatural Superpowers

INTRODUCTION

We are used to the thought of world superpowers. They are nations which have superlative military strength, including deadly nuclear strike forces, capable of destroying the human race. They dominate the world scene and preserve a very tenuous balance of power. In the last decades science fiction has brought to our imagination the idea that one day these superpowers may have to unite against superior forces invading the world from outer space. Do superpowers exist on other planets or in other universes?

Despite reports of unidentified flying objects (UFOs), there is nothing definite so far to suggest that UFOs do exist. There is much up-to-date evidence, however, that superpowers from other *dimensions* of existence *have invaded* human life. They are spiritual, belonging to realms beyond time and space. They are the Supernatural Superpowers.

This book graphically portrays how a Church of England vicar came to believe in these supernatural superpowers, experience them, and engage them in spiritual warfare. The ministry of exorcism is shown to be not only for the casting out of evil spirits from individual souls but is set within the whole panorama of our life and experiences. It is seen to be a part of the salvation of the whole man and the entire human race. In days when this part of the church's message is being assailed, the author argues powerfully that it is a vital work, a basic factor in the alleviation of suffering. Readers can draw their own conclusions on the grounds of the evidence and arguments presented in this remarkable book.

ACKNOWLEDGMENTS

This book is dedicated to all those to whom I have had the privilege and responsibility of ministering deliverance. I am most grateful to the leaders and members of St. Paul's Church, Hainault, Essex for all the help they gave me and the trust they had in me in the early days of pioneering in this dangerous yet vital spiritual warfare. I have been helped by so many ministers and owe a great deal to my wife for her constant help, sacrifice and encouragement. I wish to thank Enid Holt and Winifred Chapman for sterling work as typists and Pastor Jim Rattenbury and Rebecca, my daughter, for being patient reviewers of the script and helpful commentators on the material used. A "thank you" also to Logos publishers and their editors for helping to put together this major work and excerpts from my first attempts at writing in the United Kingdom—the book entitled *Exit the Devil*—which Dan Wooding, a Christian tabloid journalist, coauthored.

Contents

Supernatural Superpowers

1
There Is No Devil

Pat, a full-faced woman, came to St. Paul's vicarage, Hainault, East London, suffering from intense depression. She was a schoolteacher who had lived with her father. Her depressive moods began after his death.

When she came to the vicarage her neurosis was so severe that she was unable to communicate. She sat on the office sofa with her head lowered almost to her knees and sagging like a rag doll. She had been in this depressive mood for several days. Her doctor had suggested that she see me. My attempts to counsel her were useless because she would not answer my questions. I began to pray for her and, as I did, the Lord showed me clearly the details of her problems. I began to tell her all that Jesus was making known to me and that He knew her needs and was answering them.

Promise after promise came to her from the Lord through my lips. Finally I commanded her to come out of her "prison house" and break the chains in which Satan had her imprisoned.

Instead of being taken to a mental hospital the next morning, she was back at school, teaching her class of energetic children.

For me to pray for anyone to be loosed from Satan's bonds, or acknowledge Satan existed, would have been unthinkable in my college days and even during my early years as a pastor. I can still recall some heated debates with students at Cliff College.

"The devil doesn't exist!" I would shout to emphasize my belief. "It's a kid's pantomime idea." I was adamant. *There was no such power as a devil.*

That particular argument erupted one winter evening in 1954. Don and I, students at Cliff, were strolling around the nearby village of Calver, Derbyshire. I hadn't been a Christian very long and was sorting out my ideas independently of the Bible. I knew that Jesus Christ was alive and active in the world but I was vigorously opposed to the existence of any supernatural evil power. My friend was shocked. Cliff students were supposed to believe every statement in the Bible as the inerrant Word of God. I was a rebel and, despite the efforts of my friend and even the principal, I could not be converted. I left the college unrepentant and unchanged. There was no devil!

I maintained this attitude for sixteen years, through two theological colleges and ministries in Methodist and Anglican churches. But a revolution took place in my life during the next twenty years, causing the news media to "dub" me the *exorcist vicar*.

My disbelief in a personal devil was deeply rooted. It was not simply a blockage in my imagination about there being

2

some ridiculous little creature with beady eyes, horns and a tail. The whole idea of some evil life-force influencing the behavior of human beings seemed crazy to me and even dangerous. I argued that to blame the devil for our wrongdoing could reduce our sense of responsibility. I did not foresee the 1975 London court scene in which a man pleaded his innocence on the grounds that he had been "demon-possessed" at the time of his crime. I was farsighted enough, however, to see the possibilities of such excuses. We had to overcome the evil within us, rather than blame the devil, if we were really to make any moral progress.

Another serious objection to the thought of a devil was that it seemed to me to be a step back into irrationality and superstition. Progress had been possible because everything in human life had been brought within the scope of our scientific understanding. I could understand, for instance, a primitive people, without knowledge of bacteria, thinking of sickness as the work of some evil spirit invading the body; but I felt it would be a dangerous step backward for twentieth-century people to hold to the same notion. This was even more important in understanding mental illnesses.

I had suffered terribly myself from deep-seated neuroses before my Cliff College days—a sickness which led me to study psychology, including past treatment for the mentally ill. I could understand why the people of Jesus' time thought some evil life-force had invaded the afflicted person, especially when one considered the bizarre behavior of the emotionally disturbed, the seizures of the epileptic and the amazing strength of the insane. I winced with pain, however, at the dreadful medieval treatment of the emotionally disturbed as demon-possessed and therefore evil people. The practice of imprisoning the mentally sick in locked asylums had disturbed me since boyhood. I assumed in my college days and early pastorate years that rapid progress in science and medicine had made it possible to explain mental illnesses in rational diagnoses, resulting in dramatically improved medical treatment.

In my discussion with believers in the devil I had seen the caution light flash. They were in danger of returning to the practice of regarding neurosis, psychosis and brain structure disorders as demon possession. We then would open the door again to the activities of the twentieth-century versions of witch doctors, exorcists and other mumbo jumbo. I felt that medical science, which had brought definite benefits to sufferers from both mental and physical sicknesses, should never be compromised by interference from such people.

Frequently in my intellectual batterings with my devil-believing friends I launched what I considered to be a real theological rocket. I told them, "You who believe in the devil have two gods: one is good and has to be worshiped, and one is evil and has to be placated." I also argued: "Who's in charge of the universe anyway? Isn't the God and Father of our Lord Jesus Christ the only real supernatural superpower? What's a devil got to do with it all? Is he more powerful than God, the creator?"

With such strongly held opinions and insights I should have been one of the last people on earth to accept the teachings of Jesus Christ about evil and superpowers and that they are as true for our time as they were for his. In 1971, however, I began to have first-hand evidence that to understand and act upon belief in the supernatural superpowers was the key to freedom for many people living today. What brought about this change in my spiritual thinking? Possibly Elisha's prayer for a companion began to take on a deeper meaning for me—his prayer to see the light

4

(2 Kings 6:17), and also Christians praying for me. My spiritual illumination was quickened. Then, too, there was an experience as a boy.

I was a mental and physical wreck as a youngster, haunted continually by nightmares and fears. I would lie on my bed, half-asleep, imagining I was lodged inside a chasm screaming for a rope to hang onto as I fell downwards, always downwards. As fear gripped me, my parents would come into my bedroom and say, "Try to pull yourself together, Trevor."

I would fool around with ideas that my mind couldn't cope with and then blow a fuse. Once I actually imagined I was a micro-dot blowing around in a bowl of soup.

A lot of my time, between eleven and eighteen, was spent in bed, perspiring so fiendishly with fear that mother had to pile an extra pair of pajamas by my side to replace the pair saturated with my body sweat. I would shake bodily, too, sometimes so violently that the bed would rock along with me.

What really scared me was the prospect of life—*and* the prospect of death. Because I was required to run the gamut of both life and death I was filled with such dread that I suspected I would eventually drive myself insane. The idea of going insane scared me even worse.

I was ashen-faced with sunken cheeks and dark rings around my frightened eyes. I walked around with a permanent stoop due to a curvature of the spine. My mental condition hit me physically, too, since I suffered from chronic asthma and bronchitis, claustrophobia, arthritis, acute chronic sinusitis, stomach, lung and eye trouble and had to consult many specialists.

I was hardly ever at school for months on end. When I did attend I was placed at a desk near the door so that if things got too much for me, I could make a run for it. No one ever said anything when my frightened mind forced me time after time to race out of the class. I couldn't explain what was happening to me. I just ran in terror.

I spent long hours with a psychiatrist who constantly told me, "Your trouble, Trevor, is you are always looking for the answers to the ultimate questions in life. You cannot find the answers and so you have terrible basic insecurity. You are a frightened wreck." Three questions were constantly on my mind. Who am I? Why am I here? Where am I going?

The "trick cyclist," as I called the psychiatrist, analyzed me as suffering from "intense hysteria, anxiety neurosis, chronic depression, suicidal tendencies" and eventually I had "symptoms of paranoia." I would gaze at my mother and father at the meal table and be convinced they were plotting to poison me. I would look at my brothers and sisters and be sure they also wanted me six feet under the sod. I believed, too, that the doctors had a fiendish plan to get rid of me.

Medical men had written me off as a hopeless case. I remember being checked by an Army doctor as a potential National Serviceman when Britain still had conscription. He gave me the lowest possible medical grading.

Another doctor later told me, "Young man, you will only be fit for light office work as long as you live."

One Sunday night I sat in the huge echoing bowl called the Methodist Queen's Hall, Hull, situated in the heart of that Yorkshire fishing city which was my home. I made sure I was near the door. I needed a bolt hole. I was nineteen years old and still a frightened wreck.

My sister, who had introduced me to the service, looked at me reassuringly as the minister, the Reverend William Watts, a burly round-faced man, began preaching. The auditorium, with seats for two thousand, was speckled with only two hundred people but I felt he was talking directly to me as he took the Bible verse: "Come unto me all ye that labor and are heavy laden and I will give you rest" (Matt. 11:28).

That was a message that gave me hope. At last someone cared and wanted to give me some rest from my constant hell. Gradually during the next few weeks the love of Christ began to fill my heart as I attended these services. A change was taking place in my life. I felt peace smothering my fear. I had a new confidence in my step. My stoop began to straighten up. I couldn't really explain it, except that I had found Christ and knew that He loved me. I had become a Christian. I was at last becoming a whole person. I began to pray and read the Bible. Christ had started to heal my miserable life.

I didn't go forward at an appeal but I knew I had found the answer to all my questions. More than that I had found the living reality of spiritual experience.

My improvement was so great in a few weeks that I visited my psychiatrist to tell him what had happened. He seemed a hard-faced agnostic and, as I explained my change, he tore into me with devastating arguments. He ridiculed my belief in God and told me, "You must be silly to believe all that religious nonsense." I stood my ground and finally he admitted, "I am very pleased with your new-found Christian faith, Trevor. It's not an emotional prop as I first thought. You've found everything you've been looking for." Then he added with real confidence, "Goodbye Trevor, you will never need to see me again."

There still were many hurdles for me to overcome. One night I lay in bed praying to the Lord when the thought crossed my mind about becoming a preacher. I dismissed the idea as ludicrous because I still was a long way from being whole. I had a terrible medical history. But then shortly afterward the deaconess at the Queen's Hall, Sister Elizabeth Gillings, said to me, "Trevor, have you ever thought of being a preacher?"

I replied, "It sounds crazy, Sister, but I have, although it's obviously stupid."

"It's not stupid at all, Trevor," she said firmly. "You can do it."

Sister Gillings and the Reverend Watts encouraged me and soon I enrolled for a local preacher's course, my introduction into study for the ministry. Shortly afterwards I was invited to preach at a nearby Methodist church and I was on my way, but later there was a wandering in the wilderness when I needed the prayer of Elisha.

2
Seeing the Light— And the Darkness

"Lord, . . . open his eyes that he may see" (2 Kings 6:14-18). This was Elisha's prayer for a companion who was with him in the city of Dothan. The young man had cause to be afraid for they were besieged and their position seemed hopeless. The Lord answered this prayer and the man "saw chariots of fire in the mountains all around Elisha." The Lord's army had been there all the time but it needed spiritual illumination to be seen. Christians prayed like this for me because they knew that only God himself could enable me to see the existence of the evil supernatural superpowers. I needed to know both the reality of the existence of the forces of evil and the supremacy of the Lord Jesus Christ over them. I now realize that this truth can never be arrived at purely by intellectual effort. It is the work of the Holy Spirit; a revelation. It comes when we are willing, without reservation, to open ourselves to his influence.

The students at Cliff College certainly were used by God to start this revision in my thinking and my experience. They were the first people I had met who believed the Bible to be absolutely true. One might disagree with them but they had a conviction which had to be admired. They started me thinking that there might be something in their beliefs, despite what I thought.

Soon I began to develop "cataracts" over my partially opened spiritual eyes through the rationalistic approach to Christianity at theological college. The staff set out to de-Cliff me and they succeeded very well. My views that the devil was a spiritual "red herring" in the main issues of life were considerably strengthened through my studies in psychology and philosophy. Comparative religion added to this by making me very grateful that Christianity had advanced beyond primitive animism with its belief in evil spirits.

I avoided all reference to the devil in my teaching and preaching when I became a minister. If the embarrassing subject was raised I argued that the Bible's teaching needed to be reinterpreted in twentieth-century terms. Thankfully my church members seemed to have very little interest in devilish affairs. The blind led the blind. I eventually did meet real conviction amongst the church members at St. Paul's, Harlow. There biblical truth was taken seriously but it was far from a revival situation. The devil didn't really stand exposed and Christianity was the poorer for it. I have since discovered that believers are at their most fervent, dedicated and evangelistic best when conscious that they are vitally engaged in a spiritual conflict upon which the salvation of mankind depends.

In my own spiritual pilgrimage to this belief I owe much to my wife, Anne, whom I met at a Cliff College convention.

She had always believed the Bible to be true, and she held her beliefs despite real friction between us because of them. She kept me in touch with this school of thought by taking me to prayer meetings and into evangelistic gatherings. While in such meetings I felt hypocritical. I preferred my blindness. It was less disturbing. I felt she was going to the ultimate in provoking me when, one day in March, 1969, she announced that she was attending a meeting in a Pentecostal church many miles away. Her brother had become seriously ill with cancer and she was going to seek the help of Peter Scothern, an evangelist well-known for his healing ministry.

"This really is the end," I told her. "Sorry, but you will have to go alone. You will never catch me inside a Pentecostal church. It's full of poor theology and can be psychologically damaging. I volunteer to baby-sit."

A few weeks later I was sitting in a meeting conducted by Peter Scothern at Stanford-le-Hope, Essex. This came about because I had been so moved by all Anne had told me about Scothern's ministry. As this meeting began, Peter strode majestically down the aisle, straight towards me.

"There's a man here possessed by an evil spirit," he cried. I felt like crawling under the pew to escape and breathed a sigh of relief when he strode past me and grabbed a disturbed-looking youth, standing near my pew. It was all over in a few minutes.

"I am possessed! I know I am!" The young man began to shout repeatedly.

Peter Scothern cried out, "Evil spirit, I take authority over you in the name of Jesus Christ. I bind you! Come out of him, you unclean spirit!"

There was a cry, then a choking sound as the young man—a teenager—crashed to the floor (Mark 16:17). He lay there a few moments, then stood up and shouted with

11

delight, "I'm free! I'm free!"

The congregation joyously sang hymns of victory and praise to Jesus. I was riveted to the pew. I had seen exorcism exactly as it was portrayed in the Gospel stories (Luke 9:42). I had seen a phenomenon of first-century life in the scientific days in which I lived. Could it really be true? The scales were falling off my eyes. The "cataracts" were departing (Acts 9:17-18).

It was not, however, the experience of a deliverance or exorcism ministry which excited me. It was the sight of Scothern's ministry of healing which set me to seek a deeper measure of power from the Holy Spirit (1 Cor. 12:7-10). I never was an exorcist by choice. I sought the baptism in the Holy Spirit to equip me for evangelism and healing, rather than for any conflict with evil powers (Acts 1:5-8; 2:33-38). I began to attend meetings, read books, pray and fast. I studied every passage in the Bible which related to this experience. When I felt ready to receive I asked a pastor to lay hands on me (Acts 8:15-17; 19:1-6).

"Lord," I prayed, "send this power into my life."

My prayer was answered with a tremendous visitation of the Holy Spirit on May 10th, 1969. I spoke in tongues, sang in the Spirit, and prophesied, rejoicing in God (Acts 4:30-31; 10:44-46). Now I saw the glory of Jesus and the reality of His kingdom as never before. I had a new awareness of His presence and a new expectancy of what He would do. The Bible suddenly became God's inspired Word. I believed as did those students at Cliff College. It just happened. Previously I had read the Bible in "black and white." Now it came alive as if in color—three dimensions (3-D). The Word of God lived for me as thrilling, vibrant, life-transforming truth. I understood its message in a way no theological college ever could have taught me.

12

Now the Holy Spirit, who inspired the writing of the Holy Bible, was interpreting its meaning to my eager, open mind. I was a transformed person when eventually I was inducted as vicar of St. Paul's Parish Church on the Hainault Housing Estate, Essex, England, in September, 1970. I was prepared for an evangelistic ministry of real power. I was ready to minister to the sick and expected the Lord to heal them. I was not, however, prepared for the assault the devil was to launch upon me, nor the Lord's call to a ministry of exorcism.

It happened when Olive came to St. Paul's early in 1970. I first met her at a prayer meeting in our small chapel. It was a Tuesday evening and a dozen of us were met together to pray for revival. She sat there, a newcomer, pale-faced, gray haired, a slightly built lady I would guess to be in her middle fifties.

"I've dabbled in demonology and can't believe in Jesus," she said. "I talk with the devil. It's getting out of control." She paused, then, "Can you help me to be free of this evil?" She implored.

I thought her rather strange and only took what she had said half seriously. "Come along to our healing service," I invited her.

She came to our next monthly healing service, accompanied by her husband, Fred. We had barely begun to sing the first hymn when, to my amazement, Olive walked out. Later I discovered that she had seen some Bibles on a table at the rear of the church and couldn't stand the sight of Bibles which drew her like a magnet. She had destroyed several while in trance-like conditions at home.

The next day as we sat by the fire in her small but tastefully decorated council house, she told me a most amazing story. Her troubles had started some twelve years

13

previously as a result of becoming involved in spiritual seances after the death of her mother. She soon discovered that when going into a trance she actually was communicating with the devil. She told me the devil always appeared in black, was very tall, not with horns or tail, but looking like a handsome man. He wore a suit and tie.

Olive had thought at first this was a figment of her imagination but eventually she completely lost control of the situation. She began to go into trances at home when alone or in the presence of friends. The apparition, at such times, would give her supernatural knowledge about people, the future and the whereabouts of sacred objects. Always the information was accurate. Frequently when she came out of a trance she would find her home in a terrible state of disarray. Things were thrown around and Bibles lay in shreds at her feet. As these attacks increased in frequency she often would wander out of the house and once found herself several miles from home. The situation affected her family and life eventually became intolerable. She had contemplated suicide as the only possible escape.

Olive consulted psychiatrists who found her case difficult to diagnose because apart from the trances she indicated no recognizable symptoms of any known mental illness. Usually she was a normal, happy wife and mother, doing a part-time job at a nearby factory. Her husband could not explain Olive's strange actions. I told her to keep coming to church; however, I was beginning to feel the whole thing was beyond me.

A week or two later, in the middle of a service, Olive went into a trance and began walking up and down the aisle. Her eyes were fixed in a glassy stare. She was like some mechanical robot, arms outstretched and heading towards the Bible cupboard. Two stewards went to stop her but as their hands touched her she became extremely violent, cursing and blaspheming. I walked quickly to her.

"I know who you are, you man of God," she cried. "You have no power over me. I will destroy you."

She tore at me with her hands. Several men grabbed her and eventually pinned her to the floor. It was some moments before she came out of the trance, dazed, embarrassed and upset. We took her to the vicarage for a cup of tea. I needed to do some rethinking; however, I was convinced that Olive's case was similar to that of the young man at Peter Scothern's meeting. I would need to mete out the same treatment.

A week later Olive came to an evening service at my suggestion. Once again she went into a trance. I approached her with trepidation and apprehension. I had decided that I would not lay hands on her since it obviously caused her to become violent. Neither would I seek to anoint her with oil as on the previous occasion. Instead, standing a yard away from her, I addressed the evil spirits. Sensing my presence in her zombi-like state, she turned on me.

"I'm witchcraft! I'm witchcraft!" a voice vaguely recognizable as hers shouted. Then it squeaked, "She's mine! She's mine! She's mine! You can't have her. I possess her. Who are you? Who are you? Who are you?"

"I'm Trevor Dearing," I replied.

"I'll destroy you. I'm not afraid of you," came back the reply as this incredible conversation continued. But I was gaining more confidence.

"I come in the name of Jesus to cast you out," I yelled.

"Have mercy! Have mercy! I'm frightened of Jesus," admitted the voice (Mark 1:23-26).

I was thoroughly convinced there was only one way out of this situation. With complete faith in the power of God and with no doubt about the outcome, I performed my first exorcism.

"I take authority over you in the name of Jesus. You will not hurt this woman or anyone else any more. Out! Out!" I screamed. "Go!"

There was an ear-piercing scream and wailing that gradually died away. Olive fell flat on the floor as if dead. She soon thereafter stood up completely transformed.

"It's gone! It's gone!" She cried with relief as I consoled a frightened congregation.

This was not the end for Olive, however. Over a period of two years I exorcised her on twelve occasions, either in church or in her home. Through my ministry to her I learned much about the devil and the realm of the supernatural. She often was in despair until after the twelfth exorcism and then I knew that she was entirely free. All the spirits had gone and most importantly she accepted Jesus as her Savior and Lord.

Olive learned how to stand her ground against all of Satan's attempts to repossess her. She had become a radiant Christian. Possessed by evil spirits, she had suffered a great deal but the situation was used by the Holy Spirit to open my eyes and teach me many lessons that would prove invaluable later in helping hundreds of people in similar distress.

I had experienced a most dramatic revelation about the reality of supernatural superpowers. I had conversed with those real, evil, spiritual powers which had brought Olive's life to near-disaster. I had seen the power of the living Lord Jesus Christ at work today and my life could never be the same again.

3
Deliverance from Evil Powers

Had Olive been my only case of demon possession I might have thought it unique, an isolated incident, and put it behind me, concentrating my thoughts on evangelism and healing. I began to find as my ministry developed, however, that I was brought more and more into contact with these supernatural forces (Mark 1:34).

One week while ministering to the sick I heard a weird howling that sounded much like a wolf. I looked up and saw that a disturbance was taking place at the rear of the church. I hurried to investigate. A young man was running backwards and forwards across the building, his teeth bared like fangs as he shook off all efforts to restrain him. I recognized him as one who had told me about terrifying visions and nightmares. Once while in a trance-like condition he attacked a friend.

"Leave him alone," I cried. "Come out of him in the name

of Jesus."

The young man fell to the floor immediately but soon was on his feet and blessing and praising the Lord. As with Olive, this initial ministry was not the end of the man's problems. He never behaved like a wolf again but he had to receive considerable help for other needs. He also required much counseling and encouragement in a Christian rehabilitation center before his troubles were over and he was able to live a normal life.

We had many cases of people beginning to scream out uncontrollably as we ministered to them (Acts 8:7). In one case a teenage girl had to be taken from the main service and into a vestry which became a battleground until midnight. Demon after demon called out its name before being cast out of this young life. The demons argued with me, saying such things as, "Christ died for people like you but He didn't die for creatures like us."

A powerful demon told me that it had entered the girl when she was born. After being freed from her tormentors, the girl told me she had been dreadfully deprived as a child. She had spent most of her life in an orphanage. Later I learned from a psychiatrist that she had always shown marked signs of maladjustment. He gave me a very poor forecast for her future. But after the exorcism ministry, counseling and rehabilitation in a Christian family unit she became emotionally stable, successful at school and now is living a happy, normal life.

A much publicized case was that of an alcoholic prostitute from Stepney. By a strange intervening of circumstances her exorcism was actually televised. Like so many of the cases at St. Paul's, the manifestation of demon possession began spontaneously and unpredictably, without any provocation from me. I simply walked into the church before

18

the service was scheduled to begin, trying to cope with the mass of photographers and reporters who had come to see the "show." Exorcism began to be headline news. Reporters heard about my ministry and came out in force. As I walked into the church Denise began to scream uncontrollably.

She cried out, "Jesus is dead. I saw Him die."

She went berserk. I ministered to her in the name of Jesus and took authority over all demons in His name. Within five minutes she quieted, completely subdued and relaxed. The next morning she told a correspondent interviewing her that the trouble for her began when she played "ouija" (a game in which one tries to contact spirits, using letters and an indicator). She said that as a result of the exorcism she felt free and ready to begin a new life. This was overly optimistic because she still had many problems. Once again, however, my exorcism ministry proved effective in relieving terrible distress.

Critics have sometimes sought to explain this phenomenon as the effects of an emotionally charged religious meeting upon hysterical people. These symptoms, however, have occurred in the most quiet and unspectacular surroundings. I recall a doctor bringing a patient to have a chat with me in the early days of my ministry at St. Paul's before I became well-known as an exorcist. The patient was coming to talk with me as she might have done with any other vicar. As she alighted from the doctor's car, a strange thing happened. Instead of coming to meet me, she began to walk around me in a circle.

"He's too powerful," she said. "What's in me is afraid of what's in him." She wouldn't come near me.

The doctor thought he had persuaded her to enter the empty church and was amazed when, instead, she ran into the ladies' restroom, shouting, "I can't go in there. It's too powerful in there." Of course, she meant the sanctuary.

My wife and the doctor eventually induced her to leave the ladies' room and managed to get her a few feet inside the building. Immediately upon facing me again she started rolling about on the floor and shouting, "I'm seduction. I use her body. She belongs to me!"

I began to cast out the spirit of seduction in the name of Jesus and within a short time she returned to her right mind. Her problems, it transpired, had been mainly sexual. The doctor, a Christian, told me after the exorcism that she has made wonderful progress. She has been supported by Christian love and fellowship.

In view of my successes in the exorcism ministry, I asked myself, "Is this exorcism associated with one particular place, St. Paul's Church, Hainault, and not with a special meeting?"

The question was answered when invitations came to conduct missions all over England. To my surprise, I met similar manifestations elsewhere (Acts 5:16). One amazing incident occurred at Evensong in a parish church in Sheffield. As I began to pray, a man jumped up in the front pew and started screaming at me. He waved his arms ferociously. As I took a step toward him he fled up the aisle, pursued by sidesmen (ushers). They caught him in the churchyard and managed to escort him to the porch where I had just arrived. I proceeded to give him exorcism as he became more and more violent. Finally he seemed to vomit, something intangible coming out of his mouth. Then he walked triumphantly back into the church crying out, "I'm free! I'm free! I'm free!" I understand he later pursued a university course and attained a law degree.

A similar case occurred three years later when a woman interrupted a meeting, shouting, "I can't stand that man. I can't bear his eyes. He's too powerful for me. Let me out! No! No! No!" Scream after scream pierced the air.

The scene was the Sports' Centre in the small country town of Thetford, Norfolk. It was approximately ten minutes after the beginning of my "Power, Praise and Healing" meeting. I was taken by complete surprise by this outburst and the sight of an attractive, dark-haired woman, who I judged to be in her thirties, rolling about on the floor in front of me. I called our opening session of praise to a halt.

"I must minister to this poor, tormented soul," I told the congregation. "Pray to the Lord for her as I take authority over this psychic spirit in the name of Jesus."

A quarter of an hour passed as a tense spiritual conflict ensued. The evil spirit tore at the woman as it clung to her soul and body, not wanting to leave where it was housed.

"I won't go. No, I won't," it cried. "Leave me alone. What have you to do with me?"

The inevitable happened. I rendered the spirit helpless by the powerful name of Jesus, crying, "Go to the pit to await the judgment of Christ."

The poor woman relaxed into a tranquil state. When she recovered she was taken by my wife into a side room to receive further help and counsel.

The incident recalled an experience with a teenage girl who, only a few weeks earlier, had exhibited the same symptoms when confronted by my presence at the Salvation Army Citadel, Grays Thurrock, Essex. There it all had happened in a side room after the meeting. Once again someone just couldn't stand me. She tried to crawl up a wall to get out of my way when I only wanted a conversation with her.

What a strange effect I have on some people. This has happened so frequently in incidents completely isolated

21

from each other, in so many different places, that there has to be some spiritual explanation. In every case the person received the exorcism ministry, although some of these folk had known nothing about the symptoms of demon possession. I also began to hear other Christian ministers were being confronted increasingly by demonic powers in exactly the same way as I experienced. It was intensely spiritual. I was fully convinced that evil, nonhuman spiritual powers existed.

I began to sense the work of these alien powers in other situations where reaction to my ministry was not so spontaneous or dramatic. I wondered if some drug addicts and alcoholics could be possessed by spirits of addiction which controlled their lives. With this thought in mind I set about breaking the bondage that unseen spiritual powers might have over such people. The results were wonderful. I was able to give complete, instantaneous deliverance to many people where psychiatric and other treatments had completely failed. One case which particularly thrilled me was that of an alcoholic prostitute from Soho Square.

She was in a most pitiful condition, shaking from head to foot, as she came before me. She had accepted Jesus as her Savior from sin and desperately longed for a new life. She had a lovely, illegitimate child whom she loved dearly. Because of her alcoholism she had been completely unable to look after the youngster and the local health authorities had taken her into their care. The poor woman was in a terrible spiritual prison. She also was in the grip of a boyfriend who used her body. She just could not find freedom.

After she had given her life to Christ, I ministered deliverance from the grip of evil superpowers. She was liberated. Loving care and teaching by Christian friends built her faith. Happily we later celebrated the first year of

22

her new life with her little daughter, now restored to "mommy" and enjoying the anniversary party as much as anyone.

Another alcoholic, Ernie, gave his testimony to Christ's power to deliver him. He was notorious in a Scottish town both as a drunkard and a swindler. His brother, also in the devil's power, had eventually committed suicide. Ernie, however, saw a program about my work on television and traveled all the way to Hainault seeking help. He found Christ, freedom and new life for himself, his wife and family.

I shall never forget Mary, an auburn-haired, deeply wounded young woman hooked on heroin. She wanted to die and was well on her way until, as with others, Jesus set her free in her mind, soul and body.

Encouraged by my constant success, I ventured further. Could people with suicidal tendencies be subject to spirits of destruction? I launched out in a deliverance ministry to several who felt impelled to suicide against their will. They were gloriously delivered. I well remember a lady from Harlow, Essex who came to us after making several attempts on her life. She later stood up in church to share with glad thanksgiving that the impulse had ceased since my ministering to her. She was really happy for the first time in many years. She was one of many whose lives were saved by exorcism.

I also was able to bring deliverance with amazing results to people under the control of "voices." One lady had been wandering around London like a robot for many days. She and a number of others with the same problem were set free. This led me to ponder whether fears, depression and other mental torment which gripped people could actually be caused by evil spirits. Could I minister to those with cancer and other such illnesses as multiple sclerosis by deliverance ministry? The possibilities seemed endless.

I realized the dangers in the approach since I sometimes was dealing in a traumatic manner with very emotionally disturbed people. There existed two possibilities; either bringing wonderful relief or doing untold damage to their minds. Extreme care and thought were required because I was dealing with a powerful and subtle enemy. I could not treat each case the same and hope for the best. My eyes had been opened to the power of supernatural entities: therefore, my mind had to explore this spiritual realm.

Medical science had investigated the field of bacteria. Doctors did not treat patients with hit-or-miss methods. They knew their business. Psychologists had studied the processes of the mind and psychiatrists used ever-growing resources of knowledge to alleviate distress. It was obvious that those engaged in a ministry to the soul and spirit should also know their business. I had to understand what was behind all the phenomena with which I was dealing. I had to know all about demons, who and what they were, and how they entered people. I had to use the most effective ways of carrying on a warfare with them. In helping desperate individuals at the depth of their beings, I had to act with wisdom resulting from knowledge.

4
The Devil Himself

It seemed incredible but true that I, a parson who years before did not even believe evil powers existed, now was actually engaged in vital warfare against them in real life situations. I needed to know a great deal more now about the enemy I was encountering, not only to improve my strategy, but also to answer questions which still confused my mind. Were there two gods? Was I in danger of reverting to superstition? Where did medical science fit into the exorcism ministry, if at all? Could my new beliefs encourage people to blame the devil for their wrongdoings, instead of making them face up to their own responsibilities? I had to answer these questions not only for my own benefit but also to help those who were similarly perplexed and looking to me for guidance.

Jesus Christ obviously had supreme spiritual insight in this realm and I realized, therefore, that the Bible was the major authoritative source of teaching on these matters. The pages of the New Testament contain accounts of dramatic exorcisms, identical to those I had been impelled to perform. Bible study, therefore, was of paramount importance and it was logical to begin by examining the nature of the devil himself.

I discovered that the very name devil teaches one a great deal. It portrays the *character* of the evil one. The names Satan and devil really mean *hater, accuser* and *adversary.* These fiendish attributes are seen in Satan's dealings with man centuries ago.

The Bible records that the devil caused all sorts of tragedies to come upon Job in order to test his patience, steadfastness and faith even though Job was a righteous man (Job 1-2). The devil also made false accusations about Joshua, a faithful priest (Zech. 3). He made them before God, the Father. Through these trials, however, the innocence and obedience of Job and Joshua were clearly manifested. Satan's actions resulted only in the two men's vindication *as they held firmly to their faith.*

The devil, in the Old Testament, is also called Lucifer (Isa. 14:12). This name speaks of his original state as an "angel of light." He fell from grace before the universe was created. Jesus said, "I saw Satan fall like lightning from heaven" (Luke 10:18). The devil is a fallen angel, kicked out of heaven for disobeying God.

This supreme evil superpower is not simply a force like wind or electricity, but is *personal* by nature. The devil schemes, reasons, communicates and acts, as a person. He even has a body although of a different order from our own. I perceived that evil, at its ultimate, is an objective, superhuman power, able to influence humans in every aspect of their lives. The Bible teaches that Satan has organized an invasion of earth from beyond, not from another planet, but from another dimension; the spiritual realm.

The devil attempted his greatest and most prized conquest when, in a desert for forty days, he tried to persuade Jesus Christ to disobey God and become a servant of evil (Matt. 4:1-11). At that time Satan used all his powers of persuasion and offered Jesus all the kingdoms of the earth as bait to draw him into throwing in his lot with the anti-God brigade. On another occasion the devil used the disciple Peter as his mouthpiece to try to deter Jesus from obeying God by going to the cross.

"Lord," Peter said, "this should never happen to you!"

Jesus rebuked Peter with the words, "Get thee behind me, Satan" (Matt. 16:23). Jesus recognized the real source of the evil suggestion. This assault by Satan had been perfectly timed since Peter at that moment had just exhibited the most penetrating, God-given insight into Jesus' real nature and mission. Despite Satan's brilliant strategy, Jesus was not caught off guard. The enemy's plans were foiled again.

It is very important to realize that in his actions against Job, Joshua and Jesus, Satan was acting with God's permission. He was *allowed* to test and try them. Jesus was led by the Holy Spirit into the desert to be tempted by the devil. There is no question but that Satan is a rival to God. His activities are devised by his own evil mind, yet ultimately his power is limited. God can completely overrule his actions so that good will come out of them. God, because He is supreme, is able to work all things together for good for those who love Him (Rom. 8:28). We need Satan's opposition *to test our true mettle*. We, like Job, Joshua and even Jesus, need to be tested at times in order that our obedience and faithfulness to God may have real value.

It is not surprising to discover that Jesus actually warned His disciples that they too would be tempted and assailed by the devil. Satan is the adversary of Christians as he was of their Lord. His first objective is to hinder the church's work of calling men into the kingdom of God. As evangelists proclaim the Gospel, he seeks to snatch away the "seed" of belief before it has a chance to take root in the heart of the hearer (Luke 8:12). He also does his own work of sowing by planting weeds (pseudo-believers) in the harvest field of the church (Matt. 13:39). In this way he seeks to disrupt the life of the Christian community. Yet the result is that God's true children are revealed.

When I was a vicar I experienced an excessive amount of trouble in the matter of testing just when the work of God was beginning to prosper in my church. It was a harrowing experience for all of us at St. Paul's. However, as I look back, I discover that it really sifted and sorted out those who were deep Christians from those who were merely shallow (Luke 22:31). It tested genuine Christian love and drew us much closer together as a "body." In the end God made it all work together for our good. Usually it is not easy at the time to see God bringing good out of Satan's evil activities; afterwards, however, we may well say a sarcastic "thank you" to Satan for his attempts to ravage the church. He succeeds only in doing us good *when we remain faithful to our Lord.*

We are told in the Bible that the devil will invade the church through some of those who claim to be prophets, purporting to be uttering messages from God (Matt. 24:11). In this way Satan tries to obtain a hearing for his lies. This is true in the present day resurgence of prophecy in what is genuinely a movement of God's Spirit. Christians beware! We need to test every spirit to see if it really is from God (1

John 4:1-3). He will enable us to recognize the genuine prophets from the false. Praise God, there are many true prophets in the world today. By this gift of discernment Satan stands revealed and the church is built up and maintained in pure beliefs.

Satan's hatred of Christians is never more clearly seen than when he incites men to persecute the church. This was true in the first century when Christians were brutally put to death. In one of the first onslaughts of this kind against God's people, Peter wrote, "The devil prowls around like a roaring lion, seeking some one to devour (1 Pet. 5:5-9). He urged Christians to, "Resist him, firm in the faith." He was confident that this terrible suffering would have a purifying effect so that believers' faith like gold, tried in the fire and burnished, would prevail to the coming of the Lord (1 Pet. 1:7).

James taught that if Christians would resist the devil he would take to his heels and run like a dog, with its tail between its legs (James 4:7). The church would then rejoice in the victory of the Lord. The devil, in fact, only leaves the church alone when it is no real threat to him. He can afford to ignore it when it has compromised its message and mission to conform to the ways of the world.

The small groups of Christians who greeted my arrival at St. Paul's, Hainault, had posed no threat to the devil when they met together simply to get on with their own mundane business. When he began to engage in real spiritual warfare there was a dramatic change. We were harrassed, criticized and ostracized, not only by unbelievers in the locality but by newspapers throughout the land. Uninvited and unwelcome as this was, this opposition did us good. It forced a decision upon many people. Response, either positive or negative, took the place of apathy, both in the neighborhood and beyond.

In times when the church lives comfortably in the world we do well to remind ourselves of Jesus' words, "Woe to you, when all men speak well of you!" (Luke 6:26). Also, "Blessed are you when men revile you and persecute you and utter all kinds of evil against you falsely on my account. Rejoice and be glad, for your reward is great in heaven, for so men persecuted the prophets who were before you" (Matt. 5:11-12).

Any Christian who really means business with God will doubtless be assailed by the enemy (Rev. 2:10). It happened even to St. Paul. He had a tough time with what he called a "thorn in the flesh, a messenger of Satan, [sent] to harass me (2 Cor. 12:7). This assault made him very conscious of his own weakness. The result: he was driven nearer to God, to rely on His strength and, therefore, the Apostle experienced even more of the Lord's love and power. Once again Satan's efforts had the opposite effect from that which he desired. Paul was much the better Christian for his harrowing experience. The work of Satan always has this result for faithful Christians.

In my pastoral care and counseling sessions with many people I have discovered that no Christian, who is really intent on serving God, escapes satanic assaults. How privileged we are when he singles us out for deserving special attention, but how dreadful it can seem at the time. And Satan always attacks us at our *weakest* point. He may cause circumstances and situations to go wrong or try to bring our home and family life into chaos. He may strike us with sickness, fear or depression. He may even try to discourage us through Christian friends who fail us. He sometimes assails the soul during times of prayer and worship.

He may attack us in our sleep or, most insidious of all, sow seeds of doubt about our faith and love for Jesus. He is a liar and false accuser at all times (Luke 8:44). I have met Christians who doubted their salvation for a time or who thought they had committed the unforgivable sin. These are victims of Satan's lying methods. We can take hope because Satan cannot *finally* upset God's plans. There is only one God, sovereign Lord of all and He often uses Satan to work out His purposes. No one can stop God from perfecting His work in us, or prevent the establishment of His kingdom in the world.

In the biblical panorama of life the stage is not only the physical, tangible and visible world of human beings, it also is the spiritual dimension of the supernatural superpowers. We are in conflict not only with the evil within man, but with the devil and his principalities in high places. Our over-all progress will be retarded until many more people realize this to be true and act accordingly.

This insight is needed to fully understand such events as those in Northern Ireland. When we survey the terrible scenes in that country with its bomb outrages, suffering, terror and fear, it is right to blame political organizations and individuals with evil in their hearts. The Bible tells us to look beyond these human factors and to the devil himself whose aim is destruction, terror, murder and the downfall of the nations. This is true of every situation of national and international conflict. We should pay attention to the supernatural superpowers as well as to human agencies. We can successfully overcome Satan and his supernatural entities if we will heed the teaching of the Bible and apply its remedies. Men do better when, unchained by fetters of evil, they can really be themselves, free to serve in love the Lord and each other.

Christians have the insight necessary to take this action but unbelievers are in a different situation: "The god of this world, [the devil], has blinded the minds of the unbelievers to keep them from seeing the light of the gospel of the glory of Christ, who is the likeness of God (2 Cor. 4:4). Once he has blinded them he can then enter their hearts to use them to frustrate God's purposes without their knowing it or even wanting it to happen (Eph 2:2). This is what happened in Judas's terrible betrayal of Jesus. Satan actually entered Judas's heart, to use him in an issue of the greatest importance (Luke 22:3, John 13:27). But, as always, Satan overreached himself. His evil schemes were reversed in their effect and resulted in furthering God's plan of salvation since Jesus died on the cross. In trying to frustrate God's purpose, Satan, in fact, furthered it.

The devil later even managed to enter the hearts of two reprobate Christians, Ananias and his wife Sapphira, leading to their judgment and deaths (Acts 5:3-12). The devil this time was trying to cause chaos in the early church. But once again he failed to frustrate God's plans. After the death of Ananias, "Great fear came upon all the church and upon as many as heard these things. And by the hands of the apostles were many signs and wonders wrought among the people" (vv. 11-12). Satan, in trying to defraud the church, had only succeeded in enriching it.

The devil still has not given up trying. He still enters people and situations in an endeavor to hinder the work of the servants of the kingdom of God. I saw the work of Satan when, in my own ministry, an attempt was made to forbid me to preach in a country where a whole series of mission meetings had been planned. It seemed for twenty-four hours that the mission was off and we began to pray earnestly to the Lord. A miracle happened. I received full and free

32

permission to preach the gospel, heal the sick and cast out demons in that country. The glory and power of the Lord were wonderfully shown to all the church. What a beginning for a mission! Satan had done it again—unwittingly helped to forward God's work.

In all this discussion about Satan's activity in human hearts, the Bible is also clear about a real element of personal human responsibility for evil. When Paul urges us not to let the devil into our lives he is teaching that Satan's activity within us is deeply related to *our* sin (Eph. 4:27, 1 John 3:8). And Jesus lays the responsibility for sin squarely upon *our* shoulders: "For out of the heart [of man] come evil thoughts, murder, adultery, fornication, theft, false witness, slander" (Matt. 15:19).

Paul also speaks of the harvest of the *flesh* (our own nature) as immorality, impurity, licentiousness, idolatry, sorcery, enmity, strife, jealousy, anger, selfishness, dissension, party spirit, envy, drunkenness, carousing, and the like (Gal. 5:19-21). There is no doubt that we are responsible before God for everything we do and every word we utter. Yet, in sinning, we also *give place* to the devil: We put ourselves under his control and allow him the more to possess our hearts. There is no doubt that Judas's awful greed was the door through which Satan entered his heart and gained control over him.

It could be argued that when Judas was entered by Satan, he was no longer responsible for his actions. But the New Testament does not support this contention. We are reminded that Satan also desired to have Peter "to sift him as wheat" (Luke 22:31). But Peter was of a different spiritual calibre from Judas and the prayers of Jesus prevailed for him. Satan could not enter Peter because Peter, despite his failure, gave him no open door to do so.

It is obvious that Ananias and his wife *allowed* Satan's entry into their hearts. They agreed together to lie to God's people. It was their evil plan which made them easy prey for Satan. We cannot "pass the buck" on to the devil. We are never simply his puppets. In order to swing us around as he wants, Satan has to have a handle of sin to hang onto in our lives. It is through our actions that we provide that handle of sin and so allow the prince of darkness to have a place of dominion in our hearts.

We have real grounds for hope nevertheless when, even through our sin, Satan has a stronghold on us. God is the supreme judge of the extent of our responsibility. He knows how much we have been tempted and how weak we may be through our heredity and our circumstances. He is all-seeing, just and merciful, and has opened a way through the sacrifice of Jesus for us to be absolutely forgiven. If we truly repent, not only can we be forgiven, we can also be restored to life with God and freed from Satan's clutches. We can know that whatever Satan has seemingly accomplished through our failures, God will turn for good, both for us and for others because He is sovereign Lord of all.

My Bible study about the works of the devil led me to some very definite conclusions. I saw clearly that there is ultimately only *one God* of absolute power and that Satan is merely a heavenly princeling (a created being) who has rebelled against God and is now allowed a certain amount of freedom to accuse, try and test the faithfulness and steadfastness of God's children on planet earth. I realized that the furthest extent of his power is his ability actually to enter into and direct the minds, wills and emotions of human beings in his attempt to upset God's plans and purposes to reestablish his reign on this planet.

Satan can only operate to the full in those who, like him,

34

are disobedient to God and who thereby consciously or unwittingly align their wills to his end and enable him to use them. Man cannot escape his personal responsibility for his own sins which not only makes for misery and unhappiness but also enables the devil to gain access to his soul. God is supreme in the end and He has provided a way in Jesus for man's forgiveness and restoration. Because of this, Satan, try as he may, can ultimately only serve God's purposes. As God's people renounce the devil and seek the will and strength of their Lord then all things work together for good to them that love God" (Rom. 8:28 KJV).

The devil's power is placed in the right perspective when one understands these truths. Then we are not likely to overemphasize Satan's evil abilities as portrayed in the films, *The Exorcist* and *The Omen*. This overestimation of Satan's power has been the fault of many occultists and even Christians in recent years. Conversely, we are not simply to discount the activities of the alien supernatural superpowers or even deny the existence of such activities as seems to be the practice today among many materialists, secularists and church leaders so influenced. The Bible's perspective is obviously healthy and right. It certainly answers all the doubts and questions of my mind about the nature of the devil.

5
World Rulers of Darkness

There is a powerful evil spirit ruling over London. He has invaded the capital of Great Britain with filth, vice and pornography. He is delighted at the increase in the drug traffic, crime and alcoholism. For his purposes he uses men, money and machines. No area of life is outside his influence. He exerts his authority over homes, schools and courts. He even seeks access to the Houses of Parliament in order to influence the government. He would love to bring the Royal Family into disrepute. His ability to incite racial tension is a master move. Satan, his boss, is well pleased with the efforts of this underling.

Perhaps this principality is hoping for promotion to displace his superior who is responsible for bringing Britain to spiritual, economic and social ruin. He has some hope of this at present because that "ruler of darkness" is having real success in his evil work. He has been following a careful campaign plan which has worked well in previous experiments in history—sow the seeds of moral decay, spread the religion of materialism, money making, pleasure and sensuality, cause a breakdown of family life, and the nation, rotten to the core, will decay and die. It was so with the Roman Empire and other civilizations. He hopes it will work today, especially with the opportunities now available through the influence and corruption of the modern mass media—television and films—as well as education, trade unions and business corporations.

It is especially important for this principality to make the churches powerless, weak and ineffective, a sort of hobby for the respectable. He enters theological colleges to cause disbelief in the Bible—a vital tactic. He persuades Christians to compromise with the world's morals, fashions and standards. Britain has played into the hands of this ruler of darkness as also has the United States of America and both countries continue to do so. People in positions of responsibility have yielded to his influence and the spiritual atmosphere of the land is alive with evil.

What applies to London and the United Kingdom is true of every nation, city, town and village in the world. There is a satanic ruler over each one. The ultimate aim of the evil superpowers is to keep control over the world by depraving humanity. These superpowers of evil have a carefully planned strategy for causing international tension, mistrust, greed and lust for power. All of this leads to wars and rumors of wars. The evil superpowers are behind failures to reach international agreements and the consequent spread of nuclear weapons. They have been about this task of destruction since the Fall of Man let them into this human situation. Mankind has rebelled against God, turned from serving him and become slaves to the powers of evil. Consequently the blood of the slain and the terrors of the tortured cry out from the earth. These insights into satanic tactics are derived from the Bible's teaching about our human situation. Their dimensions stretch beyond human sight, taxing the imagination to the limit, and yet they are reasonable and possible.

God created the world and set man within the framework of its life (Gen. 3). He also created the heavens and other dimensions of existence. He made angels and archangels too. Angels are God's agents or messengers, especially to communicate with human beings (Matt. 1:20; 13:41; 18:10; 28:2). These heavenly beings are usually invisible to man but can make themselves known at certain times, particularly in dreams and visions. I have met many people who today describe such angelic visitations. One such person is Doris, the verger of St. Paul's. She humbly, yet sincerely, recounted visions of angels which she saw at St. Paul's Tuesday Revival Services as I was ministering to the sick.

Above these angels are archangels; the supreme created beings of the heavenly realm. Michael is one who is definitely named in Scripture (Dan. 10:13, Jude 9). Another is Gabriel who appeared to the Virgin Mary (Luke 1:26). There also are cherubim and seraphim (Isa. 6:2), heavenly nobles, whose service is mainly to surround the Lord God with continual praise and glory (Rev. 4:8,9). According to the Book of Revelation there are other heavenly beings in existence.

The Bible, by contrast, tells us about the existence of a terrible hierarchy of evil with Satan at its head. Beelzebul (Matt. 10:25; 12:24, Luke 11:15), *Lord of the Flies, Prince of the Devils*, probably is second in command. Next in seniority are the principalities and powers (Rom. 8:38, Eph. 1:21). Paul states categorically that we do not wrestle against flesh and blood but against *principalities and powers; world*

39

rulers of wickedness in high places (Eph. 6:12). These are the princelings to whom Satan has given dominion over cities, towns and countries. According to the Scriptures the whole world lies in the hand of the evil one, hence Satan could offer all its kingdoms to Jesus when tempting Him in the wilderness (Matt. 4:8,9). There are fallen heavenly princelings over London, Moscow and New York, indeed in charge of all cities, towns and villages in the world (Dan. 10:13).

It would be easy to dismiss such ideas as sheer nonsense were it not for the tragedies written on every page of human history. The human race has always dreamed of utopia—peace, prosperity and plenty. Such hopes are imprinted on our hearts. Yet, man's best laid plans have achieved nothing. Treaty after treaty has been broken and man has shed his brother's blood since the dawn of history. Scientific and technological progress which should have improved our lives has been used also for evil purposes with tragic destruction of human life, accompanied by indescribable suffering. This century the League of Nations, which didn't recognize God's supreme authority, collapsed and the United Nations likewise is proving ineffective in preventing conflicts. In our day the world is as divided as ever. The threat of a nuclear holocaust is constantly very real. Enough warheads exist to destroy the human race many times over. Economic crises give way to economic crises and tension exists all over the world. Governments rise and fall and the daily newspapers contain little but bad news.

Man, as we have seen, cannot evade his own moral responsibility, nor the challenge which he must face in solving his problems. It is not fanciful to recognize that behind these failures, as well as behind terrible "natural" disasters and other catastrophes, are personal, evil powers scheming and planning the downfall of man. To comprehend the total human predicament, it is essential to read and interpret today's news reports with a full understanding of the tactics of the evil superpowers in the world today. We cannot actually prove the existence of these evil forces because we normally accept reality through our five senses: sight, hearing, touch, taste and smell. Any person or anything real to us, whether our husband, wife or a building, has to be apprehended through one or more of these senses. The existence of nature and the material world does not have to be proved. They obviously are there. Proof is not so easy, however, when we consider spiritual realities such as supernatural superpowers. These, by definition, are not available to our senses. We cannot in the same manner hear, see or touch them. Yet, throughout history mankind has reached beyond the prison of his senses to contemplate spiritual horizons beyond that of his present life where all his longings might be fulfilled.

It would be a very biased view indeed to assert that existence is limited to a human being's sense of experience. Even an atheist would surely have to pause before saying that man must live entirely within these limitations. Science, especially physics, seems at the present time to be stretching the realms of possibility; constantly enlarging the area of that which is real to the senses. The telescope has brought previously unknown planets within the sight of our eyes. The microscope has revealed forms of life previously too small for us to see. Bacteria very much affected human life even when they couldn't be seen. Spiritual realities likewise will always be beyond our sense experience, yet they are real to millions of people and many of these believers are among the most intelligent, able and mature

41

people in the world.

Faith is the sixth sense through which the spiritual dimension of life becomes real (Heb. 11:1). Christians live within the laws, conditions and limitations of other human beings, yet they have horizons beyond them. They know that such events as the rising of the sun and the birth of a baby can be scientifically explained but they still thank God for the gift of another day and for the miracle of childbirth. So too, when adverse events take place, they see in them the hand of the devil and his evil subordinates. They penetrate beyond physical appearances to the spiritual dimensions of life which are so profoundly affecting human history. They see the ultimate cause of man's predicament and are thankful that they know the ultimate answers to his needs (Eph. 3:10, Rev. 2:10,13).

6
The Little Devils

The vast spiritual horizons which I had become aware of since leaving Cliff College enabled me to view the panorama of human existence with new penetrating insight. I began looking through the events of life to the spiritual realities underlying them. I no longer saw life in three dimensions but in four. I grasped the depth of biblical teaching as never before and learned a great deal about the devil and his subordinates.

It was now clear to me, from the Scriptures, that it was not the devil himself who I was exorcising from the lives of people. I was certain also that it was not the principalities and powers who had possessed the unfortunate men and women I had given deliverance. The invaders were either demons (little devils) or "unclean" spirits (Luke 4:33). Although these were the lowest orders in the kingdom of evil, I knew from my own experience, as well as from the

Bible, just what devastating effects they could have on human minds and bodies.

The incidents recorded in the New Testament show that there are many varieties of evil spirits and that they can affect our lives in all manner of ways. The Lord Jesus Christ taught that they enter man through the soul, especially where a spiritual vacuum exists (Luke 11:24-26). My Bible studies showed me also that people who expose themselves to satanic influence through willful, continual, evil practice could actually become controlled by these demonic forces.

The first area they affect is the spiritual life where they can cause havoc with a person's experience with God; worship, prayer and love for the Lord can become completely disoriented. Demons can even produce para-normal religious abilities such as clairvoyance, mediumism, fortune-telling, false tongue-speaking, disturbing visions and tormenting spirit voices (Rev. 16:14, Matt. 24:24, Acts 16:16). The afflicted person can sometimes be affected morally, being dominated by uncontrollable passions, lust and "unclean" spirits. False feelings of guilt and rejection by God can cause considerable misery while genuine spiritual life is held in a viselike grip. The victim is in terrible spiritual bondage, totally unable to relate properly and adequately to God or man (Acts 8:9-24).

The ultimate in this spiritual condition we call possession. The word possession does not actually occur in this connection in the Greek of the New Testament. Instead, the demonically afflicted people are described as "demonized" or "having a devil," meaning they are literally ruled by an evil spirit or demon. From the home it establishes in the soul, the demon can control whole areas of the victim's life. In the most dreadful state of all, that of multiple possession, sufferers are hardly ever themselves.

44

The Little Devils

A typical biblical instance is that of the man of Gadara (Mark 5:1-20). He had apparently worn no clothes for a long time and could not even live in a house but spent most of his time in graveyards. When he saw Jesus he cried out, fell down before Him and said in a loud voice, "What have you to do with me, Jesus, Son of the Most High God? I adjure you by God, do not torment me" (v. 7). The spirits frequently had made this man so violent that he had been kept bound with fetters and chains. Superhuman strength had enabled him to break the chains. Everyone feared him. Jesus asked him his name and received the amazing reply, "My name is Legion; for we are many" (v. 9).

The symptoms had definite spiritual overtones. He reacted violently to the presence of Jesus. He had supernatural knowledge about the nature of our Lord. His voice was obviously under the control of the powers which pleaded with Jesus not to cast them out. His behavior was beyond his control frequently as the powers that ruled him gave him phenomenal strength and directed his steps to where they wanted him to go. His preoccupation with graveyards, the place of the dead, had spiritual overtones.

On another occasion when Jesus was in a synagogue he met a man who had an unclean spirit (Mark 1:23-28). The man shouted, "What have you to do with us, Jesus of Nazareth? Have you come to destroy us? I know who you are, the Holy One of God (v. 24). Jesus rebuked him, saying, "Be silent, and come out of him!" (v. 25). We read that "The unclean spirit, convulsing him, and crying with a loud voice, came out of him" (v. 26).

Once again we see that although there were psychotic elements in this man's behavior, the symptoms of possession were basically spiritual. Demon possession is a deep-seated *spiritual* sickness with *spiritual* symptoms, *spiritual* causes, requiring a *spiritual* remedy.

The Bible further shows that once they have become enthroned in the soul, demons can not only cause serious spiritual problems, but they can create chaos in the mind and the body. This is because we are not simply machines but complex psychosomatic organisms.

We are "fearfully and wonderfully made." Our minds, for instance, cannot be placed in a bottle and labeled. When the mind becomes sick the source of trouble cannot be discovered by X-ray examination. Our minds are spiritual (metaphysical) entities. We all know that our mental condition can have far-reaching effects upon our bodies. There is scarcely any limit to the physical symptoms which can be produced by our minds. Our spiritual life is basic to both our emotional and our physical health, having far-reaching repercussions on our whole beings.

When the Holy Spirit enters us nothing but good can result. Through His influence on our lives we can be made whole, not only spiritually but also in our minds and bodies. I was completely healed of deep-seated mental and physical sicknesses through my experience of conversion. The Holy Spirit began to rule my life and pervade my whole being with His healing power.

Conversely, evil spirits can quite definitely cause symptoms of physical sickness and prevent the proper functioning of parts of our bodies. For instance, we all are aware of the handicaps endured by those born deaf. One difficulty is that they cannot communicate easily with others because they never have heard sounds in order to imitate them. The deaf and dumb were around in Jesus' day (Matt. 9:32). He healed some of them by treating them as cases of demon possession. Once he astonished a crowd by shouting at a deaf child, "You dumb and deaf spirit, I command you, come out of him, and never enter him again" (Mark 9:20-29). At this the youngster went through convulsions and seemed to have died. But Jesus took him by the hand and lifted him up. Obviously Jesus had been addressing a spirit which had heard and obeyed His command. The child was cured. Jesus, however, did not treat all cases of deafness the same way.

On one occasion he put his fingers into a man's ears and cried out, "Ephaphatha" ("Be opened"), and immediately he could hear again (Mark 7:32-35). Deafness caused this man to have a speech impediment which was healed at the same time. Jesus, therefore, made a distinction between healing which He ministered when He knew that the condition resulted from a physical cause and deliverance from evil spirits when the affliction was of demonic origin. He always knew the difference.

Matthew records that Jesus once treated a blind and dumb man as a case of possession (Matt. 12:22-29). This man had both his sight and speech fully restored and the remarks of the crowd indicate that an exorcism ministry had taken place. They asked, "Does not this man (Jesus) cast out devils by Beelzebul, the prince of devils?"

A comprehensive study reveals that Jesus did not treat every blind person as possessed by evil spirits. Blind Bartimaeus received his sight through an act of faith in Jesus' power to heal (Mark 10:46-52). So, too, did a man born blind (John 9:1-12). He was helped to receive healing through having his eyes anointed with clay and then washing in the pool of Siloam. These men were healed not exorcised.

Not only deafness and blindness but also physical infirmities were sometimes exorcised and at other times healed. Mary Magdalene is said to have been healed of evil spirits and infirmities (Mark 16:9; Luke 8:2). Seven devils had been cast out of her and the indication is that the demon possession and the infirmities were closely linked. This connection between demons and infirmities is clear also in the case of the woman whom Jesus healed in the synagogue on the Sabbath day (Luke 13:11-17). This woman obviously had some sort of deformity of the spine and could not straighten herself. When Jesus saw her He laid hands on her and said, "Woman, you are set free from your infirmity." Immediately she was made straight and thanked God. It is significant, however, that Jesus asked the Pharisees the question, "Shouldn't this woman, a daughter of Abraham, whom Satan has bound for eighteen years, be set free on the Sabbath?" Jesus' pointing to the spiritual origin of the deformity revealed it to be a satanic binding.

Sometimes Jesus ministered healing rather than exorcism to those who were lame or infirm. Seemingly identical symptoms could have very different causes and the effectiveness of Jesus' ministry shows that He always understood the area in which He was operating.

In my ministry I have had to exercise the same care. I have known physical symptoms to be entirely relieved by exorcism. Olive, out of whom I cast twelve spirits, had a severe spinal affliction which caused her intense pain and resulted in her dragging her left leg. These infirmities had baffled specialists for many years but they disappeared after she had been set free from the devil's power. This is only one of several cases I have known where the casting out of spirits of infirmity has resulted in the definite healing of physical complaints. In most cases, however, it has been a healing ministry in which my experience has brought relief to hundreds of infirm people.

Epilepsy in many of its aspects is a mysterious illness with all sorts of possible physical and psychological causes.

Sufferers often have other related afflictions and disabilities with which to cope. It is certain that Jesus healed a boy who suffered from this illness by casting out an evil spirit (Luke 9:37-43). The incident began with a man emerging from the crowd shouting:

"Teacher, I beg you to look upon my son, for he is my only child, and behold, a spirit seizes him and he suddenly cries out; it convulses him till he foams, and shatters him, and will hardly leave him."

As Jesus was going to the boy the demon threw the youngster to the ground and tore at him in a terrible manner. Jesus rebuked the unclean spirit and healed the boy.

In my ministry at St. Paul's, Hainault, I was called upon to help several epileptics, including Trevor, a man suffering terribly from this illness. He had no more seizures after I cast out an epileptic spirit. When treating this illness I realized that, as with many sicknesses, it might have a physical rather than a spiritual origin. Sensing that it was of a physical nature, I ministered for the healing of brain cells and structures.

If ever I am uncertain about the origin of any illness, I ask the patient if he knows from medical evidence whether the sickness has a physical cause. If the answer is affirmative, I minister healing to the affected part, praying that the Holy Spirit will drive out sickness and heal nerves, tissues, cells, fibers and muscles. When an affliction has a spiritual origin, I invariably use the powerful name of Jesus to cast out the evil spirit. I have witnessed amazing results in the alleviation of physical pain and distress through this aspect of the exorcism ministry.

The New Testament also ascribes the cause of some mental illnesses to the activity of evil spirits. The man of

Gadara, as we mentioned earlier, was a case of multiple possession. Obviously this had a terrible effect on his mind and today he would no doubt have been diagnosed as psychotic or schizophrenic. The same applies to the man who cried out in the synagogue, "What have you to do with us, Jesus of Nazareth?" (Mark 1:23-28). People behaving in like manner today, in extreme cases, would be labeled temporarily insane. Psychiatrists would seek to treat them as medical cases and use all their skills to bring relief. In many cases in my ministry I have seen the cause of the emotional disturbance to be demonic. Exorcism has saved these people from deep distress and contributed a very great deal to their restoration to normality.

It is a serious mistake to treat all cases of psychosis or neurosis as demon possession. Jesus taught that people could be bruised and heartbroken as well as Satan's captives. He was referring to sicknesses, wounds and bleeding, pain and distress in the very depths of a person's being. He was really pointing to the need for inner healing of the personality, the subconscious mind. Psychiatrists have shown that neurotic and psychotic conditions, such as irrational fear, chronic depression, and schizophrenia frequently have their origin in emotional bruising and personality breakdown.

Sensitive ministry for inner healing, sometimes of the memories, is needed in such cases. Certainly traumatic exorcisms, especially when prolonged or constantly repeated, could cause serious harm and further disturbances to people suffering from these deep-rooted sicknesses. Jesus always knew the difference between demonically caused emotional disturbances and those mental illnesses which arise from other sources. We who, in His name, minister to people in deep distress must exercise the same discernment, wisdom and sensitivity.

People today are still being affected by demonic powers. They try bravely to live normal lives, despite the terrible spiritual, physical and mental disturbances which these invaders can produce. They definitely are helped by drugs and other medical remedies. Ultimately they can be healed but only when we use the means God has placed at our disposal.

My study of the Bible enabled me to grasp the underlying principles of demonic possession and my knowledge of psychology helped me to understand how evil spirits could affect every part of a person's life. Thus, I had a clear picture of both the extent and the limits of the powers of evil spirits—a knowledge which is absolutely essential in a ministry of exorcism. Since grasping these truths I have ministered with new conviction, certainty and confidence in freeing people from evil forces with definite, abiding results (Luke 4:18, 19). Much genuine happiness has resulted from my exorcism ministry—a ministry which has brought many scores of people who knew not what to do to turn completely to the healing power of Jesus Christ.

7
Satan's Territory

God began to bless my ministry at St. Paul's Hainault, in a wonderful way in 1971. Hundreds of people were converted to Christ in our small back street church. Many miracles of healing took place with dramatic deliverances by exorcism. Satan, however, had some very deceitful tricks which he employed to prevent the growth of my ministry. He wanted me to be blind to his reign over the occult realm. He even planned to get me involved in it.

I had never given much thought to spiritism, either during my years in theological college or in my ministry in the church. What I knew of it, however, did not attract me. There seemed to be something intrinsically somber and sinister in seeking to contact departed spirits. I did not relish sitting in a darkened room awaiting a medium's message. The thought of automatic writing and clairvoyance also left me cold. Some of my friends had attended seances and been terribly distressed at predictions about catastrophes in their families. One or two mediums I had met in the course of social gatherings had seemed cranky, overpowering women. Jesus warned, "You will know them by their fruits" (Matt. 7:15-23). So I kept clear.

Soon after my arrival in Hainault I had a most unusual interview with one of my parishioners. He was deeply Christian and utterly dedicated, loving and sincere. He told me a most impressive story about a "sitting" with a famous medium soon after the death of his wife.

"Vicar," he said, "she described my wife in minute detail. There could be no mistake. She was in touch with my wife. The medium gave me several lovely messages from her, including details about our life together which the medium could not possibly have known.

"It meant a great deal to me and assured me that my wife had survived beyond the grave. The medium also told me that on my birthday my wife would send me some spiritual flowers. Sure enough, on that very day I awoke to find my bedroom filled with a most beautiful, heavenly scent and glorious colors covered the ceiling. It was lovely."

I was most impressed. Could my previous views about spiritism have been mistaken through ignorance? No one at that time showed me that this leading of people into occult involvement, through natural grief, was the most insidious and cruel trick the devil could play upon unsuspecting people.

Satan's next strategic move was to send to St. Paul's spiritists who had heard of the healings at the church and came to give me encouragement. I was lonely for fellowship with others engaged in the healing ministry. Could these people be allies? They spoke to me of their own healing abilities, of the work of Harry Edwards, and even invited me to speak about healing at the Ilford Spiritualist Church. I went along, eager to share with them the Gospel of Jesus Christ. The meeting was most memorable for the hearing they gave me and their obvious delight that an Anglican vicar was laying hands on the sick. They were most impressed with what I said.

"He is really one of us, although he puts things differently," said the leader to the second-in-command.

"He really ought to be given details about how to join the National Federation of Spiritual Healers," the leader said to another spiritist.

I had mentioned in my address my departed brother-in-law, George. One medium said she had seen him standing beside me all the time I had been speaking. She urged me to see her as soon as possible for a "sitting."

"Have you a guide to the other side?" she enquired.

"Yes. Most certainly," I replied.

"Is he powerful?" she asked, looking very excited.

"Supremely so," I declared.

"Do you know his name?"

"Yes. Jesus Christ! I know Him very well. All my healing ministry is in His name. He heals. I'm His servant."

She showed surprise when I said, "I wish you knew Jesus, too, then you would realize that there is no need of anyone else to guide you."

I had known no fear, only power to witness to these folk who were sincere but, I decided, misled. The sinister feeling I had always had—a feeling of darkness about spiritism—was reinforced through my experience in their church. A few seemed very relieved that healing could be ministered in such a "natural," free and open way as I had described at St. Paul's.

I recognized three of the spiritists at my next healing

service. Two of them accepted the Lord Jesus Christ as their Savior and renounced all connections with the occult when they saw the wonder of the healing power of Jesus in this Anglican Church. They told me of their terrifying experiences as they had tried to become mediums. One had been tormented by horrific visions and suffered definite spiritual disturbances. She needed exorcism. Eventually she found release for her soul and the fulfillment of her needs in the baptism of the Holy Spirit.

They were the first of the many converts from spiritism which occurred in my ministry. In the glorious love-permeated atmosphere of our Tuesday evening meetings at St. Paul's, they had found true hope, peace and joy in Jesus. It is sad that some Christians are so suspicious of those who have been converted to Christianity from involvement in the occult. Some Christians even are afraid of these new converts. Occultists are often sad people in all kinds of spiritual trouble. They are people for whom Christ died. When they have found Him, they frequently are greatly gifted and extremely sincere in His service.

In my ministry I continually meet Christians who tell me hair-raising stories of how they became demon possessed through involvement with spiritism. One of these, Robert Lee, has since become my main helper in dealing with demonized people. He learned so much the hard way in his own attempts to become a medium. He wrote to me describing his horrible experiences.

"It was April 9, 1961," his letter began. "I had a big job, a big salary, a big office and a big problem. I had been searching for God, but as I sat at my desk after lunch, I watched my hand pick up a pen and start to write. I didn't want to write. With an effort I could have stopped it for a time, but I didn't put forth that effort.

"My hand started to write out the name of my *guide,* or was it yet another *guide.* I was becoming confused. It was a very long name with a lot of letters, and half way through the spelling I was told we would finish writing it tomorrow. It sounds hilarious now, but it wasn't a bit funny then. I felt I just couldn't take it anymore.

"I had only snatches of sleep for two months. As I lay in bed, wide awake, whispering voices prepared me for the next ordeal to prove I was worthy of God. I had submitted myself to all these whispered preparations in night-after-night and day-after-day sessions, being told by a voice to go on some meaningless journey or talk to some particular person and *it would be all right.* It had not been all right at all. My colleagues were beginning to give me strange looks. I was fighting to remain normal at work and home. There was not only that voice but also clear colored pictures like color television in my mind. I saw them in a rectangular panel to the right of dead center. My arms and hands were starting to do things I had not told them to do. I remember particularly the horror of even drinking a cup of tea. As soon as I decided to pick up the cup, it picked up itself and came at my mouth as my arm moved out of my control.

"All the wonderful promises the voices had made to me just were not worth it. I couldn't keep up the pace. Even as I thought this I knew *they* were hearing my thoughts. 'God,' I murmured, 'I'm just no good to you. Let me go back to a normal life.'

"The answer to my pleas was dynamic. A force seized my shoulders and thrust me down onto my blotting pad. How long could I hold on? 'God,' I began weakly. But a voice inside my mind said, 'This isn't God. . . . This is the devil.' The voice added, 'And now I'm going to drive you mad.'

"I could feel the thing inside me moving in for the kill.

What an utter fool I had been. I had tried to find God outside the beloved Savior Jesus Christ. This landed me in the hands of the devil—like a fly tied up in a spider's web.

"My wife and I had been investigating spiritism in which her family had some non-active interest. My wife soon realized I was getting deeply involved and urged me to take it more easily. Tuesdays I was at the spiritist church in Ilford for the 'healing' services. Sunday night I attended the worship service. But the big attraction was visiting mediums. I seemed to receive message after message from alleged parents and friends who had 'passed over.'

"Looking back, I should think ninety percent of the messages were so general as to be inept. For instance, 'I've got a kind old man wanting to speak to his son. That's you, sir, with the blue tie. He says you must not worry about mother. She is at peace and sends you all her love.' Folk still sorrowing for lost relatives often swallow this sort of thing as I did. Ten percent of the messages I received, however, could not be easily explained. No doubt the devil has some genuine information to give to cause people to become further involved.

"I introduced the ouija board to my family and friends, even encouraging my children to participate. We got an active response with a lot of information, some which could not have been faked easily, such as the name my father called my mother (Meg) which no one else knew but me. At this moment of reality I knew I had been deceived. Fragments of nearly forgotten Scripture came back to me and I knew I had separated myself from God in denying Jesus Christ. I knew I had sinned utterly. I had loved things which were an abomination to God. What possible hope could there be now?

"I got up and walked over to my office window. The thing

inside me was moving up and down. It could influence my movements, thought and speech. It was like having another pair of hands on one's steering wheel. How could I fight it? Then the thought came to me of the night before and filled me with dread. My family had practically given me up. I just had to find help. But where? My doctor? He had been giving me loads of sleeping pills which had had little effect. I had refused to tell him why I couldn't sleep. A hospital? I could just imagine trying to explain! Suddenly I realized I was possessed. I remembered enough Scripture to convince me that I was demonized. The thing inside me actually reacted when I thought of demons. I asked myself, 'What is the opposite of the devil?' A church came to mind and I thought, 'I must find a church.' "

Robert Lee, my correspondent, did find a church and was completely delivered from this evil power through the effective exorcism conducted by some Presbyterian ministers. After this, all traces of psychological and emotional disorder disappeared. He was a free man.

I had no part in Lee's problem or his deliverance which had taken place twelve years before I met him. Mercifully God had kept me from any involvement in occult activities. The devil had tried to mislead me but, as always, his power is limited. God is sovereign and the devil, in the end, serves God's purposes. So Satan's attempts to sidetrack me into spiritism had the opposite effect. It opened my eyes to the main source of the problem of evil spirits in people's lives.

Robert Lee's story needed no verification but the majority of those who needed deliverance in my own ministry proved that beyond dispute. In nine out of every ten cases their problems began with occult, especially spiritist involvement.

A headmaster once phoned me and asked, "Trevor, can

you come to the school at once? Some boys have confided in me that they have been playing ouija. They started out treating it as a game but now they are terrified. Two of them have been in trances and one has attacked his friend with a knife on the instructions of his dead grandfather. They feel possessed. It's grown out of control."

I hastened to the school where I prayed over the boys for their complete deliverance. They had no further trouble.

Another remarkable instance was called to my attention one night when I arrived home to find a rough looking cockney standing on my doorstep. He was shaking life a leaf. With him were two equally-built men, looking very agitated.

"Can you help my friend?" The question seemed to explode from one of the men's lips. He added, "He has attacked his wife and might kill her unless you can do something for him. Something must be done tonight."

Slowly the story unfolded. The wife was a nurse on night duty. The husband had been alone and, feeling somewhat bored, decided to play ouija to see if there was anything to it. To his horror voices began to pound through his brain and eventually one spirit began to take control of his actions. He became violent and when his wife came home he attacked her. Since then, a fortnight previously, he had been unable to work and was in a terrible emotional state. He was desperate to find relief from voices and visions. He was not a churchgoer or in any way religious and had not seen a doctor for years. He had no history of psychiatric disorder.

There was only one thing to do. I exorcised him in the name of Jesus Christ, casting out three evil spirits. Like others during this ministry, as in the days of Jesus, he became *as one dead*, lying at my feet (Mark 9:26 KJV). Eventually he arose a free man.

Exorcism ministry needs a special gift—the *discerning of*

spirits. This is the God-given ability to feel the presence of God or the presence of evil in something that is said. It enables the gifted person also to feel correctly the presence of evil in people or places. Jesus knew what was in man. I recall an occasion when a lady from Southend was found wandering about London at the dictates of voices. She was able to communicate with spirit guides who had used her to heal but she nearly went mad as night after night she had nightmares, visions, heard voices, and went through uncontrollable actions. No psychiatrist seemed able to help her; but Jesus did.

I have had dealings with many who have tried to become mediumistic or psychic healers and who have become possessed in the process. This is not surprising since the whole concept of mediumship is to open the soul to spirit-guides so that they actually possess the seeker. The object of the exercise is to be able to communicate spirit knowledge or healing power to other people. When in contact with spirits, mediums sometimes go into trance-like conditions as the spirit "on the other side" takes control of them. Their hands may be used for automatic writing, their eyes for visions and so on. It is not difficult to see how so many people who had engaged in this sort of activity become psychologically disturbed. The whole business is very unhealthy from both a Christian and a psychological viewpoint.

We can illustrate the occult process which results in possession by drawing a parallel with a television set. This instrument is sensitive in picking up pictures and sounds which would not otherwise be heard or seen by those sitting in the room. We can tune into different channels for various programs.

Our human spirit also is an ultra-sensitive apparatus

designed to contact that which otherwise would be beyond the realm of our senses. We are meant to turn in to the "God-in-Christ channel"—the Holy Spirit—which is healthy, wonderful, fulfilling and a source of good things to enrich our lives.

Occultism, however, is tuning into another channel—just as real—but which is the domain of the devil. Once on that channel we are in terrible danger, for it is not easy to change and, even if we manage to do so, we may still get a lot of interference. The Christian exorcism ministry, in one of its aspects, is a dramatic re-tuning of the soul to the channel where we experience the Holy Spirit of God. Only good results can follow when we are on the right channel.

God has warned us that occultism is a "no-go" area for man. The perils are so great that God's command is backed by extreme sanctions in order to deter us. We are warned: "Do not learn to imitate the abominable customs of those other nations. Let no one be found among you . . . [who is an] augur or soothsayer, or diviner, or sorcerer, no one who casts spells or traffics with ghosts or spirits, and no necromancer. Those who do these things are abominable to the Lord, and it is because of these abominable practices that the Lord your God is driving them out. . ." (Deut. 18:9-13 NEB).

King Manasseh's sins are described as: "He practiced soothsaying, divination and sorcery and dealt with ghosts and spirits" (2 Chron. 33:6 NEB).

God has commanded: "Do not resort to ghosts and spirits, nor make yourselves unclean by seeking them out" (Lev. 19:31 NEB). And, "I will set my face against the man who wantonly resorts to ghosts and spirits, and I will cut that person off from his people" (Lev. 20:6-7 NEB).

Occultism and spiritism are no new phenomena. They go

back to animism, the primitive religion of pagans. Ultimately they are from the same source as witchcraft, magic, superstition and evil of all kinds. Occult, spiritual forces are still used as a source of supernatural power to work in man, either for his destruction or his supposed well-being. Occultism is not a contact with God's heavenly realm but its fallen counterpart, the devil's domain. Thus Satan counterfeits all that is wonderful and good in the gifts of the Holy Spirit. There are occult revelations and clairvoyance, counterfeiting the Holy Spirit's gifts of knowledge. There are psychic healings, counterfeiting divine healing; fortune-telling counterfeits prophecy, and even devilish miracles can be worked and devilish tongues imitate the precious holy gift of Pentecost (Matt. 24:24, Rev. 16:14). Satan uses all these things to bait the curious, the superstitious, and sincere seekers after the truth into his snare and prison house.

Such is the subtlety of Satan that he has been able to invade even the Church of England with occultism and spiritism. This has been mainly through what is called the Church's Fellowship for Physical and Spiritual Research. This organization has published its areas of interest as clairvoyance, clairaudience and telepathy and other spiritist preoccupations. It has links with so-called Christian Spiritualism (a contradiction in terms) and has engaged well-known mediums for its activities. It has become "respectably" established, numbering bishops among its patrons. Sincere but misled seekers after spiritual phenomena have become members of this Society holding meetings on church premises with church members constantly encouraged to attend. How subtle Satan is!

Psychically gifted people are met on the pages of the Bible. It is interesting to see what happend to them. In the

Old Testament there is the story of the witch of Endor (1 Sam. 28:1-20). This medium is described as having a familiar spirit. She had a psychic, supernatural ability to know King Saul despite his disguise. He asked her to predict the outcome of a battle by consulting the dead prophet Samuel. A spirit appeared and the whole incident ended in the tragic death of the king in battle.

The use of the term "familiar" spirits is revealing. They are evil spirits (not human) who are familiar with a dead person's appearance, habits and life. They imitate the deceased in order to lead mourners astray—into occultism. Such experience is both real and supernatural. It also is false. It deceived my friend at St. Paul's, Hainault, who thought the medium was in touch with his wife and he became interested in the occult. Thousands have been tricked by this most cruel of the devil's deceits. Mediums, in their seances, are possessed by these familiar spirits. Familiar spirits also have been known to visit bereaved people without invitation.

Our loved ones, who have died in faith, are at peace and rest in the Lord (Heb. 4). They can be left safely in his everlasting arms until we join them in heaven. They have more than survived. They have eternal life—life of a new quality. Whenever we worship we join with angels and archangels and all the *company of heaven* in praising God and magnifying His holy name (Rev. 5:7-11; 7:9-12). The church triumphant is with the Lord. We believe in the communion of saints although now separated from us by the narrow stream of death. There they pray for us and some Christians believe it is fitting for us to pray for them. Personally, I can hardly think of any need they can have for us to pray about, such is their joy. Often I ask Jesus to give my departed mother my love as she with me awaits the consummation of all things at the Lord's return. Then all God's people will be reunited with wonderful new spiritual bodies (1 Cor. 15:20-58, 2 Cor. 5:1-9).

It is very significant that the New Testament records meetings between the early Christian evangelists and psychically endowed people. A man named Simon had used sorcery and amazed the people of Samaria, claiming that he was someone great (Acts 8:9-13). Everyone paid attention to him, saying, "This man is that power of God which is called Great (v. 10). And they listened to him because he had bewitched them with his sorceries for a very long time. Philip did not congratulate him or join in fellowship with him. Simon was converted when he saw the true and more powerful workings of the Holy Spirit. He saw the lordship of Jesus through miracles of healing and exorcism, done in His name. He repented and was baptized, converted by the preaching of the gospel.

Paul also met a magician at Cyprus (Acts 13:1-12). He was named Elymas, the sorcerer. He opposed Paul, seeking to turn the proconsul from the faith. This man was exposed when Paul, demonstrating the superior power of Jesus, shouted, "O full of all guile and all villainy, you son of the devil, you shall be blind, not seeing the sun for a time."

Immediately there fell upon him a mist and a darkness and he went about seeking someone to guide him by the hand. Then the proconsul, when he saw what had happened, believed, being impressed by Paul's teaching about the Lord. Here is an instance of Satan's overplaying his hand, whereby he furthered the purposes of God.

Another psychic person mentioned in the New Testament was a slavegirl who brought a great deal of money to her owners through her ability to tell fortunes (Acts 16:16-18). She also had the occult power of divining, with psychic insight into the source of Paul's powers. The demon in her told her that he was a servant of the most high God. Paul cast out the spirit of divination. This girl was young.

Recently there has been great interest in Britain in psychic children. Attempts have been made to put them on television shows. These children have received the occult power usually through the interest or involvement of their forebears back to the third and fourth generation. There are records of children in the London area being baptized into the occult of witches.

The early Christian evangelists were often confronted by occultism as the devil sought to impede the progress of the gospel. The result always was victory for Jesus. At Ephesus many people who had practiced magic brought their books together and publicly burned them as the Christian message struck home to their hearts (Acts 19:19).

There are even indications in the New Testament that people can be possessed by religious spirits. Our Lord once was accused of having one as he claimed to be the Son of God (John 7:20; 8:48). He, of course, was God incarnate, possessing the Holy Spirit of God. Jesus did not deny that possession by a religious spirit was possible for others. I have cast out misleading religious spirits at St. Paul's. Those possessed by them, quite definitely, had spurious religious thoughts, activities and abilities not verified by Scripture. In the Bible we meet people who had supernatural powers which were not from God, and there are many such people around today.

In my experience which agrees with biblical teaching, I have found the following to be occult activities which can lead to involvement with evil spirits:

1. The use of charms.
2. Astrology—studying our stars.
3. Black and White Magic.

4. Blood covenants which involve exchanging blood through wounds, with the invoking of religious powers.
5. Fortune telling—by whatever method.
6. Clairvoyance.
7. Yoga and Kung Fu which when practiced fully involve the concept of spirit guides, fighting a battle through their respective devotees. The human fighters are merely puppets, portraying the spiritual battle going on behind them.
8. Fetishes.
9. Chain letters.
10. Spirit healing.
11. Superstitions of all kinds.
12. Rod and pendulum.
13. Levitation.
14. Witchcraft whether "black" or "white."
15. Divining (water, etc.).
16. "Hard" drug addiction and alcoholism.

It is extremely important for us to realize that occultism, in all aspects I have listed, is a growing phenomenon of life today. The last decades have seen an almost incredible occult explosion. This is in stark contrast and reaction to the science and rationalism which are supposed to be characteristics of this age. In fact, human beings are incurably religious and there can be no more of a religious vacuum than a psychical one. In these days of much puerile churchianity, Birmingham, England has nineteen covens, at least. The satanist movement flourishes in Britain and America. In 1971 only 400 deacons were ordained in the Church of England. In the same year 450 ministers of Satan were ordained in one week in America.

Places, as well as people, can be the habitation of spirits

when occult or evil activities, such as seances or murders, have taken place there. I must admit to being very skeptical about benevolent, benign spirits wandering purposely about houses. All human spirits are, or should be, at rest in the Lord, therefore, there must be something devilish about such manifestations. Sometimes, however, a lurking presence may result from orgies held on the spot centuries before when the place might have been part of a forest. "Haunting" and occultism usually go hand-in-hand and affected places must be reclaimed from the devil's domain to the kingdom of God.

The most difficult area for undiscerning people to see occultism is where it most closely resembles the spiritual gifts of tongues, interpretation of tongues, faith, miracles, knowledge, healing, prophecy, discernment of spirits and wisdom (1 Cor. 12:7-11). These have been manifested for over fifty years in Pentecostal denominations and more recently in the great revival of spiritual life in the traditional churches, the charismatic movement. The use of these gifts, when genuine, has let to the advancement of God's kingdom and much glory to the Lord Jesus Christ. It should not surprise us, therefore, that Satan counterfeits the best gifts of God in the same way that money counterfeiters find it more profitable to reproduce a twenty pound note rather than a one pounder because reproducing the larger note is more profitable. However, it is of crucial importance to recognize what is genuinely of God. Jesus spoke somber words when he said, "On that day many will say to me 'Lord, Lord, did we not prophesy in your name, and cast out demons in your name, and do many mighty works in your name?' And then will I declare to them, 'I never knew you; depart from me, you evildoers' " (Matt. 7:22-23).

The Bible states categorically that no one speaking by the

Spirit of God can call Jesus accursed and no one can say, "Jesus is Lord," but by the Holy Spirit (1 Cor. 12:1-3). It is not meant here merely the verbal statement "Jesus is Lord," but also that which comes from a depth of conviction and insight into the divine nature, mission and Saviorhood of Jesus. Occult practitioners do not believe, when pressed, these scriptural truths about Jesus even though they may have a picture of Jesus hung on the wall of their home. We should always be sure that the ethos in which the gifts are being exercised brings glory to Jesus in worship, praise, adoration, aspiration, joy, gladness and light. One has only to compare a seance to a charismatic praise service to see and feel the difference.

A Holy Spirit ministry is always within the context of the Body of Christ, the Church. It has, as its ultimate aim, not simply the healing of the body, but the salvation of the soul from sin through faith in the sacrifices of the Lord Jesus on the cross. Its message will be entirely biblical, including such themes as heaven, judgment, hell, forgiveness and Christ's victory over Satan. A true prophet will not disobey God's laws by trafficking in spirits and ghosts. There will be only one guide on the other side, Jesus Christ; only one healing and saving Spirit, the Holy Spirit. In the end the real test of a true Christian ministry is manifested by: "Is this person preaching the gospel? Is he or she bringing people into the kingdom of heaven?" The power of Satan may satisfy the curious and bring temporal benefits but the devil never will venture to destroy his own work by winning souls for the kingdom of God.

How I thank God that he opened my eyes to the reality of the kingdom of darkness! I could never have understood the main cause of demon possession without this knowledge. It would have been a case of the blind leading the blind. Now that I've seen this truth, I take every opportunity in newspapers and on radio and television to warn people not to trespass on Satan's territory, looking for spiritual treasure. It has been my great privilege for several years to lead many straying, troubled and even possessed souls back into the pathway of peace and into the joy of a true dynamic, life-giving religious experience which can be found only in Christ Jesus, our Lord.

8
Divine Combat

Satan's reign on earth ended when Jesus was crucified. It was the Friday of Passover, A.D. 27. The news of the outcome of this titanic struggle between the two great supernatural superpowers was first made known to the world on the following Sunday, the day Jesus rose from the dead. Chosen witnesses were commanded to declare to the ends of the earth the stupendous fact of Satan's downfall (Matt. 28:16-20). They were to invite all mankind to enter into the freedom Jesus had won for them (Mark 6:15, Luke 24:47). The Bible enables us to grasp the sequence of events which led to this amazing reversal of the balance of supernatural power on our planet earth.

In the beginning God had limited his sovereignty by giving freedom of will to every created being, both in heaven and on earth. All were given the ability to choose between right and wrong, good and evil (Gen. 2-3). They were free either to obey or disobey the Lord Jehovah. God did not create robots, but *persons*. He desired to have a deep relationship with them through a free act of their will. He would not force them into a love relationship because the essence of love is a free response to the beloved. The potential for good was wonderful; the potential for evil, terrible; but it was a risk love had to take. This is the deep truth portrayed in the story of Adam and Eve in the Garden of Eden. As this story clearly shows, Satan had already rebelled, coveting to be as God himself. He then appeared in the guise of a serpent and tempted man also "to be as God." Lured by this ambition, man yielded to Satan's power.

So man almost completely lost his experience of God as this evil supernatural superpower tightened his grip upon the human race. Idol worship, paganism, occultism and superstition, often with the terrible rituals of human sacrifice, became the order of the day. Mankind became: "dead in trespasses and sins," "fulfilling the desires of the flesh and of the mind," living under the control of "the prince of the power of the air [Satan]" (Eph. 2:1-5 KJV). For "all have sinned and fall short of the glory of God" (Rom. 3:23).

The Bible is the only book in the world which not only describes man's fall but also God's rescue operation.

God looked from heaven and saw "earth," a planet He had given mankind to inhabit, swinging in space. On it He had created a unique species in His own image and intended for an abiding deep fellowship with himself. Now He saw the human race groping in spiritual darkness, in a constant state of rebellion against Him, cut off from a godly life, doomed, dashed and bound for hell. He saw men shackled in chains, imprisoned by a fallen heavenly princeling—the devil. Humans had sold themselves into Satan's hands through their sins. Principalities, powers and spiritual hosts of wickedness in high places ruled over them (Eph. 6:12). Evil spirits harassed, tormented and afflicted their souls while demons sought to inhabit their minds and bodies. He saw the occult realm, Satan's domain, falsifying and counterfeiting his precious gifts, seducing and enticing men through their curiosity and desire for spiritual power. Multitudes had been led further and further away from Him. Satan had conquered the world.

God still loved this world very much (John 3:16). He would not give it up. A rescue operation had to be undertaken—the greatest and most glorious that ever could be conceived. One person of the Trinity, another supernatural superpower, paid to save mankind from all this terror. We cannot know the whole counsel of God. There are truths beyond the limit of our small minds to grasp. We can, however, understand the essentials of what this divine mission involved. God has shown them to us in the Bible and they make sense.

First in God's rescue operation, the precious freedom He had given man could not be violated. A free response must still be at the heart of it.

Second, the victory would have to be won within the dimension of human life itself. The battle must be before the eyes of men on planet earth. Men and women would then realize their terrible plight, see their real enemy and know he was defeated. They would understand how their heavenly Father, out of love, had saved them and called them back to himself. Since God's children were made of flesh and blood, "He himself likewise partook of the same nature, that through death he might destroy him who has the power of death, that is, the devil. . . ." (Heb. 2:14).

"The reason the Son of God [Jesus] appeared was to destroy the works of the devil" (1 John 3:8).

Third, this great rescue act would have two dynamic and

profound aspects; it would deal with the heart of man's problem—the evil within him; it also would deliver him from the evil outside himself, the devil and all his works. The Savior of man would become a perfect sacrifice for the sins of the world and by doing so deal a death blow to Satan (Heb. 10:10). No human being could possibly do this. Even the most holy man living would still be a sinner, powerless against the superhuman forces of evil. Help was needed from outside, from heaven itself. A superpower would have to enter the human arena. God chose the Israelites and prepared them to receive this Savior of mankind.

When all was ready the decision was taken in the council halls of God and by a free act of love, Jesus, God of God, Light of Light, Very God of Very God, stepped out of eternity into time and space (John 1:1-18). This is no once-upon-a-time story. It was when Augustus was the Emperor of Rome, Herod was King of Judea and it was the year of the first Roman census (Luke 2:1-2). It happened in a particular place, Bethlehem, in the Middle East (Matt. 2:1). God used a young Jewish virgin to be the vehicle of His becoming a human being (Matt. 1:18-25). At a certain, chosen time, in a carefully selected place,

"Our God contracted to a span
Incomprehensibly made man."

Charles Wesley

He could now be seen, heard, and handled (1 John 1:1). He had entered the sphere ruled by the devil for a specific task, to save His people from their sins and deliver them from the hands of the evil one.

On the stage of history, with the dust of earthly soil upon His feet, Jesus the super Power, came to offer us peace with God (2 Cor. 5:18-19). He spoke of God's offer of reconciliation in terms like that of a father welcoming home his long, lost

74

son (Luke 15:11-32). In that parable the wayward young man had sunk to the gutter, eating in a pigsty. Then he came to his senses. He decided to go home and, without excuse, seek the forgiveness of his father. When he arrived he had hardly begun to get out the first words from his mouth when his father ran to him, fell on his neck and kissed him. His status of sonship was immediately restored fully. "This," Jesus was saying, "is what God is like in His dealings with sinful man." This offer of forgiveness to the penitent was a constant theme on Jesus' lips.

He didn't only speak. He acted. He showed God's forgiving love, not only by His words, but also by His deeds (Luke 5:17-26, 7:36-50). His associations with spiritual outcasts such as Mary Magdalene (a prostitute) (Luke 8:1-2), Zaccheaus (a tax collector) (Luke 19:2-10), and the Samaritans (regarded by the Jews as *beyond the pale*) (John 4:9), brought him into direct conflict with church authorities (Luke 15:1).

"You eat and drink with sinners," they accused (Luke 15:2).

"The Son of Man came to seek and save the lost," Jesus retorted (Luke 19:10). It was the religious scandal of the time.

If Jesus were around today He certainly would spend much of His time seeking the lost in Soho and other places where iniquity abounds. Former strippers and prostitutes, male and female, might well be among His traveling companions. He would be offering new hope to "drop-outs," drug addicts and alcoholics—casualties of modern society. It is almost certain that He would have little to do with the churchianity and religiosity which often goes on in His name today. In Jesus' ministry people mattered even more than principles. Contacts with spiritual down-and-outs were much more important than formal acts of worship. The Pharisees, the most ardent religionists of the day, were the objects of his most scathing criticism (Matt. 23:13). He called sinful men and women from the highways and byways of life into the kingdom of God (John 8:1-11).

From one angle it was this scandal which aroused the hatred of officialdom, making his execution an urgent necessity. From another angle, Satan was at work, using these men to avert Jesus' threat to his kingdom (Mark 14:12-25). Above all, the mastermind was God, working out His plan of salvation for mankind.

John the Baptist had it "weighed up" from the outset. When he first saw Jesus he shouted, "Behold, the Lamb of God who takes away the sin of the world!" (John 1:29). Later Jesus revealed God's plan to His disciples, saying, "The Son of man must suffer many things, and be rejected by the elders and the chief priests and the scribes, and be killed, and after three days rise again" (Mark 8:31-32; 9:31; 10:33).

The drama unfolded as He walked towards the cross. He freely chose to lay down His life for His brethren (John 10:1-18). As He ate His last meal with His followers, He took the wine and gave it to them with the words, "This is my blood of the covenant, which is poured out for many for the forgiveness of sins" (Matt. 26:28).

His death was necessary to save mankind. So the day came when a hysterical mob, a group of religious hypocrites, a cowardly politician and a bank of drunken soldiers, nailed Him to the cross (John 19, Luke 23, Matt. 27). Man's sin has never been more visible. But amidst the horrors of it all we see *the love of God*. As men and women have gazed at the cross they have found *a love stronger than their sin*—a love that has drowned their sins in its unfathomable sea. Jesus said, "Greater love has no man than this, that a man lay

76

down his life for his friends" (John 15:13).

What a depth of love; to die so that friends may live. This Jesus did. We see on the cross a love greater than this. Jesus did not die for His friends—*He died for His enemies*.

"God shows His love for us in that while we were yet sinners Christ died for us" (Romans 5:6-8). While we were enemies against God, we were reconciled through the death of His Son. By grace have we been saved.

Jesus actually prayed for His murderers: "Father, forgive them; for they know not what they do" (Luke 23:34). All mankind was included in that prayer. Such love is too high for us to fully comprehend.

John Wesley, founder of Methodism, wrote:
"O, love, Thou bottomless abyss,
My sins are swallowed up in Thee.
Covered is my unrighteousness,
Nor spot of guilt remains on me,
While Jesus' blood through earth and skies,
Mercy, free, boundless mercy, cries."

In Isaiah 53:5-6 we read the words that another composer, G.F. Handel, set to music in his oratorio, "The Messiah":
"He was wounded for our transgressions,
he was bruised for our iniquities. . . .
All we like sheep have gone astray,
We have turned everyone to his own way;
And the Lord hath laid on Him the iniquity of us all."

We know that He bore our sins in his own body on the tree (1 Pet. 2:24). Millions of people have found this to be true in their own experiences as they have freely and unreservedly surrendered to God's love, unconditionally accepting what He has done for them. Sin, which has its origin within us, and allows the devil to get us in his grip, now has an effective answer in the blood (sacrifice) of Jesus. No science, technology, medicine or psychiatry could have done this for us. A spiritual need had to have a spiritual remedy. To see this truth and apply this remedy can revolutionize the life of men and nations.

On the other front, Jesus was absolutely triumphant over all the spiritual forces of wickedness. He encountered them right at the start of his mission. Straightaway there was in the synagogue a man with an unclean spirit. He cried out saying, "What have you to do with us, Jesus of Nazareth? Have you come to destroy us? I know who you are, the Holy One of God" (Mark 1:23-27).

To the amazement of the crowds Jesus immediately cast out one of Satan's minions. He was constantly engaged in such deliverances. The incidents are too numerous to study in detail, but in every case the issue was never in doubt (Mark 7:26, Matt. 8:28-34, Luke 11:14-26, Mark 5:1-20). The evil spirits always acknowledged His authority over them. It was at this stage that the sheer authority of His status prevailed. It was a continual manifestation of the power of the kingdom of God which Jesus was inaugurating. It opposed, superseded and overwhelmed the kingdom of Satan.

The devil had to launch a counter-offensive. He first used some of the Jews to accuse Jesus of being a spy. "It is only by Beelzebul, the prince of demons, that this man casts out demons" they said (Matt. 12:24-28, see also Mark 3:22). "He's in league with the devil" (Matt. 9:32-34). This was a thrust at the very heart of Jesus' mission.

In defending himself, Jesus taught a basic lesson about His victory over the powers of evil. He said, "Every kingdom divided against itself is laid waste, and no city or house divided against itself will stand; and if Satan casts out Satan, he is divided against himself; how then will his kingdom stand? And if I cast out demons by Beelzebul, by whom do your sons cast them out? Therefore they shall be your judges. But if it is by the Spirit of God that I cast out demons, then the kingdom of God has come upon you. Or how can one enter a strong man's house and plunder his goods, unless he first binds the strong man? Then indeed he may plunder his house" (Matt. 12:25-29).

This is a commentary on the running battle Jesus fought with Satan's minions and depicts his constant victory over them.

Satan had yet to be dealt with and in order to take him on, Jesus had to fight a battle to the death. He spoke of this in terms of a ransom that had to be paid. "For the Son of man also came not to be served but to serve, and to give his life as a ransom for many" (Mark 10:45).

This later was reiterated by Peter in his first letter when he wrote: "You know that you were ransomed . . ., not with perishable things such as silver and gold, but with the precious blood of Christ, like that of a lamb without blemish or spot" (1 Pet. 1:18-19).

Jesus' life was the ransom which had to be paid to set us free from the powers of evil. Jesus set His face toward Jerusalem to die on the cross. The Savior of men did not resist (1 Pet. 2:18-25). He was led like a sheep to the slaughter. A most revealing moment came when He cried out from the cross, "It is finished!" (John 19:30).

It could have sounded like a cry of failure and despair. Humanly speaking, it looked as if He was defeated and His life was over. The Greek word used for *finished* means *completed* and denotes *a cry of satisfaction*: the shout of a man who had perfectly and absolutely finished His work to the very last detail. So Jesus had fulfilled His mission. It also was a cry of triumph for Satan had been vanquished. He had brought all his forces into action to engulf Jesus but had failed abysmally. Jesus, by dying, had won a victory not only for himself but for the entire human race. It had been achieved at our level, sharing our nature, at the scene of the conflict. Satan's reign was over. A victory shout rang out through the heavens! "It is finished!"

This victory was clearly demonstrated by Jesus' resurrection on the third day. The extent of that victory is portrayed by His ascension to heaven, to the exalted status He forever enjoys.

Paul prayed that people would begin to understand "what is the immeasurable greatness of his power in us who believe, according to the working of his great might which he accomplished in Christ when he raised him from the dead and made him sit at his right hand in the heavenly places, far above *all rule*, and *authority* and *power* and *dominion* and above *every name that is named*, not only in this age but also in that which is to come" (Eph. 1:18-23; see also 3:10).

"When he ascended on high he led a host of captives, and he gave gifts to men" (Eph. 4:8).
"He disarmed the principalities and powers and made a public example of them, triumphing over them in him" (Col. 2:15).

The word *triumph* quite definitely has military associations. Can you imagine the streets of Rome when they were celebrating a great military victory? How would they welcome their conquering hero? They did it by giving the general the honor of a triumphal procession. On the appointed day the streets were lined with crowds of cheering, excited people. The hero, on his stallion, sword upraised, was the first to come into sight. He was at the head of the procession. Behind him came all his commanding officers and the troops, glittering in finery. They were followed by chariot after chariot, full of jewels, treasures and garments, the spoils of the defeated foes. Finally came the conquered kings, trailing abjectly along in chains, heads bowed. They were objects of ridicule and scorn. Jesus enjoyed such a triumphal procession as He "ascended" to heaven with all the spoils of the occult realm.

He led captivity captive! This battle, fought on the hill outside Jerusalem in A.D. 27, has repercussions through every dimension of life on the universe. It is a cosmic victory, a heavenly fact. It still, however, has to be fully manifested for the victory has yet to be fully implemented on earth. This is because God still preserves the original freedom He gave His creation and, therefore, still allows even the defeated foes some measure of activity, although their end is certain. Beleaguered garrisons of evil continue to hold out like the Japanese in the jungles in the Second World War who didn't know their government had surrendered. Men also may freely avail themselves of that which has been done for them but only when they surrender to God are they free from Satan's power.

The real triumphal procession will be manifested on earth before our eyes and in our dimension at the return of the Lord Jesus Christ in power and great glory. Then we shall really see the completeness and absoluteness of Jesus' victory, won for us through the seeming weakness and failure of the cross. The victory will then not only be visible to the eyes of the faithful, but manifested to all mankind. Jesus foretold how certain signs of the times would indicate the nearness of His coming. Many Christians believe these to be now taking place and that the Lord soon will take His expectant people to be with Him in glory.

The Book of Revelation teaches that the devil will then have one last, terrible fling before finally being destroyed and cast into the place "prepared for him and his angels"

81

(Rev. 12:9-12, Matt. 25:41). Jesus, the supernatural superpower, is victorious.

How grateful I am that when my eyes were opened to the reality of the devil and all his works, I saw more clearly the extent of Jesus' victory over them. Since then, with millions more, I have seen Christianity as the most vital force in the universe. I have been able to sing to Jesus with profound conviction.

"Alleluia sing to Jesus
His the Scepter, His the throne,
Hallelujah, His the triumph,
His the victory alone!
Hark the songs of peaceful Zion
Thunder like a mighty flood.
Jesus out of every nation
Has redeemed us by His blood.

William Chatterton Dix

9
The New Generation People

Satan has been defeated! The powers of evil which engulf human life can be swept away. There is hope for mankind. Goodness, justice, love and truth will prevail. The Lord Jesus Christ is on the throne of the universe. When I realized the truth of these dynamic facts my life was revolutionized. I saw the task of the church as vital, urgent and critical. My ministry also was revitalized as I gave myself entirely to the task of evangelism, healing and exorcism (Luke 9:1-2, Matt. 10:1). It did not deter me that I came to be regarded as "outside the respectable." I threw in my lot completely with those who were determined to drive back the forces of evil, reclaim the lost and bring the reign of Jesus to men's hearts. In the Bible these farsighted people are described as a "new generation"—a unique race, those who have been twice born (1 Pet. 2:9). Their first birth was through normal, natural parentage; their second through a life-transforming spiritual experience of the power of Jesus (John 3:1-8, 1 Peter 1:3).

When anyone becomes a Christian he is a brand new person. He is not the same any more. A new life has begun (2 Cor. 5:17)! The release accompanying this new birth is graphically expressed by Charles Wesley in the hymn "And Can It Be That I Should Gain?":

"Long my imprisoned spirit lay
Fast bound in sin and nature's night.
Thine eye diffused a quickening ray;
I woke—the dungeon flamed with light!
My chains fell off, my heart was free,
I rose, went forth, and followed Thee."

The life of these new generation people pulsates with meaning, purpose, peace, liberty and joy as they engage in their God-given task of powerful ministry within the kingdom of God. The Lord Jesus taught that in order to enter this kingdom it is necessary to repent (Mark 1:15, Luke 13:3). This involves renouncing both sin and the devil.

"I renounce the devil and all his works, the vain pomp and glory of this world with all the covetous desires of the same and the sinful desires of the flesh so that I will neither follow nor be led by them" (1662 Prayer Book, Baptismal Service).

This act was not simply to be a momentary impulse, but a life-long attitude of mind, emotion and will. New generation people have deliberately transferred from one side of the supernatural conflict to the other and they are very conscious of the fact that the transfer fee which bought their freedom was not paid in money, but in blood, through the sacrifice of Jesus on the cross.

Christians, in obedience to their Lord, have to urge mankind to renounce the devil and believe on the Lord Jesus Christ. Sadly this belief often has been represented by the

84

church as simply the formal recitation of a creed, or as mere intellectual assent to Christian truth, a "train of ideas in the head." Sometimes it has been conceived as something that happens when one begins to go to church. However, faith in Jesus is much more than any of these; it is an utter abandonment of one's self to the person of Christ. The believer becomes Jesus-centered and Jesus-oriented. He loves Jesus, prays to Him, cleaves to Him, obeys Him, worships Him and looks forward to being with Him in eternity forever.

This confession of Jesus as Lord at this depth, and with this result, springs from the inspiration of the Holy Spirit. Ultimately it is His work to make men Christians. He has committed the task of proclaiming the reality of man's slavery to the devil, Christ's victory, and the essentials of salvation to the new generation people. This work has gone on for nearly two thousand years and is as necessary as ever today. As I realized the urgency of the task, and asked Jesus to fill my inadequate life with the power of the Holy Spirit, I soon began to see hundreds of people experiencing the joy of the second birth. They were brought from the domain of the devil into the life of the kingdom of God (Col. 1:13-14). There can never be a greater thrill in life, never a more meaningful service to humanity, than that of bringing man out of darkness into the Lord's marvelous light (1 Cor. 12:3).

Repentance and faith are the inner attitudes required for salvation. Jesus instituted the rite of baptism as the outward sign that this new life has begun (Matt. 28:18-20, Acts 2:41; 8:36-38). It is said of Martin Luther that whenever he was assailed by the devil he shouted at him, "I've been baptized!"

The Lord, in fact, chose baptism because it dramatically portrays the fundamental ingredients of the salvation He has procured for mankind. The root meaning of the verb "to baptize" in the Greek is *to dip* or *to immerse.*

In the early church new Christians were taught that their going under the water symbolized their death to the old life and identified them with Jesus' death upon the cross (Romans 6:3-11). In the same way their coming up out of the water pictured their rising to newness of life with Christ—new people, under new management.

Two other important benefits of Jesus' salvation are portrayed in this glorious act of water baptism. First, as water is associated with cleansing of the body, so baptism symbolizes the complete washing away of sin from the soul through the blood of Jesus. Second, as water speaks of our natural birth through the mother's uterus waters, it symbolizes the spiritual birth of a believer into the race of new generation people, and foreshadows the further baptism by the Holy Spirit.

Little wonder the devil hates baptisms. Faced with them his position is rather like that of the Pharaoh who chased Moses and his people across the desert to the sea (Exod. 14:15-31, 1 Cor. 10:1-2). The Israelites escaped his clutches as they went across dry land with the Red Sea banked up on either side of them. When the enemy tried to cross, the water saved the Israelites by drowning the Egyptians. God's ancient people were rescued through water, symbolically by baptism. Satan knows that as God's new generation people go through their waters, he cannot follow after them. He simply stands gnashing his teeth on the far side. He has lost more of his slaves.

Repent! Believe! Be baptized! These have always been the fundamental, absolute and bare essentials of the Christian clarion call to the world. When really heeded with the heart, mind and will, and with reality, the Holy Spirit is at work bringing into being another brand new person (James 2:19). Another new life has begun.

10
The Divine "Turtle"

New generation people have a new status in the spiritual realm. They share a position of reigning with Christ (Eph. 2:4-6). They are freemen in the city of God, "blessed . . . with every spiritual blessing in the heavenly places" in Christ Jesus (Eph. 1:3). They now sit with Christ in heavenly places. He has made them worthy to share all the treasures of those who belong to the kingdom of light (Rom. 8:17, Eph. 1:18-19; 2:19). God has rescued them out of the darkness and gloom of Satan's domain and brought them into the kingdom of His dear Son (Col. 2:12-13; 3:1-4). In this position of privilege they have a unique place of protection. For them the promise holds true.

We "who dwell in the shelter of the Most High, [and] abide in the shadow of the Almighty, will say to the LORD, 'My refuge and my fortress, my God, in whom I trust' " (Psalm 91:1-2). God is our refuge and strength, a rock and a fortress against the attacks of the enemy (Psalm 31:1-2).

Little wonder the New Testament writer confidently declared that overwhelming victory is ours through Christ. Nothing can ever separate us from His love (Rom. 8:37-38).

This spiritual security is for both mature Christians and their children. Believers, "little ones," stand under the protecting umbrella of the faith of their parents and of the whole church. Eventually, however, in order to enter fully into their heritage, the "little ones" also must experience the new birth. God has no grandchildren.

This place of privilege which Christians enjoy does not mean that they will never be exposed to Satan's assaults upon their souls. The evidence of the Bible, history and personal experience show that Christians still will be tempted. Because they are God's people, rowing against the tide of evil in the world, they will experience more temptation than unbelievers can ever know. The advice given to them in this situation is to "Resist the devil and he will flee from you" (James 4:7). Yes, Christians will be tempted but they have no need to be overwhelmed (1 Pet. 3:16-18).

Christians also will be persecuted. During Satan's earliest assaults upon the church Peter wrote: "Your adversary the devil prowls around like a roaring lion, seeking someone to devour. Resist him, firm in your faith . . ." (1 Pet. 5:8-10).

Jesus forewarned His disciples that they would be persecuted and He actually told them to *rejoice* in their sufferings, recognizing them as a mark of good spiritual pedigree (Matt. 5:10-12).

God apparently allows new generation people periodically to be persecuted in order to test and purify their faith (1 Pet. 1:6-8). The Bible teaches that even though the devil may thrust Christians into prison and slay them, they will be vindicated in the end by their heavenly Father (Rev. 2:10).

Christians may even experience a "hammering" from Satan. Paul knew this experience when he complained about "a thorn . . . in the flesh, a messenger of Satan, to harass me." He was really brought low, and three times he pleaded with God to get rid of it. The Lord's reply to him is of abiding significance for all Christians:

"My grace is sufficient for you, for my power is made perfect in weakness" (2 Cor. 12:7-9).

God has provided His people with a spiritual armor with which to ward off Satan's attacks. If we wear it we shall still be found standing even when the devil has done all he can to hurt us. The armor is the belt of truthfulness, the breastplate of right living, shoes to facilitate speed in preaching the gospel of peace, the shield of faith with which we can stop all flaming darts of the evil one, the helmet of "salvation" and the sword of the Spirit (the words God has spoken) (Eph. 6:13-17). This, of course, is a picture of a Roman soldier in battle dress. It is also a picture of a Christian squaring up to the legions of the devil. The new generation people are soldiers in an army, a theme taken up in many "battle-cry" hymns. The following is from Onward Christian Soldiers by the Reverend Sabine Baring-Gould:

Onward, Christian Soldiers, marching as to war.
With the cross of Jesus going on before.

The words of this hymn pulsate with meaning and significance when one's eyes arc wide open to the reality of spiritual warfare. Christians are called to fight a battle in which they know they can never ultimately be defeated. Christ is risen!

As we set out to engage in this conflict, it is of vital importance to realize that we are not involved simply in one-armed combat. It was to the church, the new generation people collectively, that Jesus promised, "On this Rock I will build my church, and the powers of death [hell] shall not prevail against it" (Matt. 16:18).

Christians cover and protect each other by their mutual faith. It is true that in this battle, "Together we stand, divided we fall." The church is more like a Roman *turtle* than a conglomeration of solitary soldiers. The turtle was a battalion of soldiers standing side-by-side, back-to-back, shield-to-shield, until they were a massive wall of metal—a human tank. Those in the middle turned their shields to face upwards, providing a metal roof to protect against arrows from the sky. Thus the soldiers were protecting themselves and each other. Once formed, this solid metal mass would move steadily towards objectives in enemy territory, invincible in their complete solidarity. Christians, too, must join together in unity, forming "prayer turtles" and cutting across denominational lines in every place where the spiritual battle is raging.

The words of the hymn writer, Reverend Gould, must always be a reality: "Like a mighty army moves the Church of God," as we steadily march against the positions the enemy now occupies, both in the world and in human hearts.

Opposing an offensive such as this, Satan's tactics are always to divide the church, to set one Christian against another, to stir leaders into party strife, to cause heresies and schisms. We experienced this strategy of the enemy at St. Paul's Church, Hainault, as we moved out in spiritual warfare. Satan even sent false prophets among us to cause confusion and division. Christians who, by their words and deeds, divide the church are acting as Satan's emissaries (Matt. 7:15-23). Drastic disciplinary action must be taken against them (1 Cor. 5:5). They might even have to be expelled in order to preserve the vital unity of God's people

(Titus 3:10).

It follows from our picture of the turtle that the church, the turtle of God's true new generation people, is a place of real protection from the ravages of Satan. Add to this the Lord's promises to his people and the knowledge we have of his victory and surely no Christian, in deep involvement with others, need be afraid of the devil and all his works. Unfortunately I have met many frightened Christians in my ministry. This is sad because fear, the opposite of faith, is a vital loophole in our defenses. Once a Christian becomes afraid he is very vulnerable to Satan's power.

This was so in the case of three Christians who telephoned my vicarage in abject terror. My wife, Anne, answered the call and was told, "We have just passed a house where a seance was in progress. A great black cloud seemed to come out of the door and envelop us." The young man reporting the incident was in such terror that he could hardly get his breath. Anne could hear his teeth chattering.

"Ask Trevor to come immediately to give us deliverance," came the urgent plea. My wife explained to them their standing in Christ. She told them that they could claim the victory which was theirs in the name of Jesus.

"Go back," she said, "and tell all the evil to go from your friends and from the area in the name of Jesus. We will be praying for you."

A few minutes later the young Christians phoned again, shouting with delight, "It worked! It worked! Praise the Lord!"

On another occasion a Christian wrote me along the following lines: "I am very frightened. I have recently moved into a new flat and have discovered that the people below are holding seances. I feel strange tremblings coming over me and cannot sleep."

I explained to my correspondent the authority all Christians have through faith in Jesus. Then I added, "I hope to hear soon from a medium saying, 'Please help me. A Christian is praying above me and I can't get through to the occult.' "

So often Christians seeking help have simply been frightened. They have been fearful of places or of people involved in the occult. The devil's power over them has been directly in proportion to the extent to which they have feared him. Christians who resist him find he soon flees.

An old Chinese fable can teach us some truth. It is said that once upon a time a town was being harassed by a terrible dragon. The more the townsfolk fled from it, the larger it grew until it became as large as a mountain. One day a boy, armed only with a stick, came to town and to the amazement of the folk volunteered to kill the dragon. He had realized the secret of victory and set out with confidence. Eventually he returned with the news that the dragon was dead. How had he killed it? He had simply walked closer and closer towards the enemy, completely unafraid. As he did so it grew smaller and smaller until he was able to pick it up, put it in the palm of his hand and kill it with his stick. Shades of David and Goliath? That in principle demonstrates how we should be aware of our authority and victory in Jesus Christ and points the way to deal with the devil.

Christians who treat the devil in this way are secure from his ravages. They are secure but not immune. It is a sad fact that sometimes Christians do let Satan influence them to such an extent that he is able to overcome their solitary defenses and enter into them. This was true of Ananias and his wife, Sapphira in the early church. They undoubtedly were members of the early Christian community yet they took themselves out of "turtle" formation when they agreed together to cheat the church. Peter had to ask them, "Why has Satan filled your heart to lie to the Holy Spirit . . . ?" Their end was disastrous (Acts 5:1-11).

It seems that in the case of Galatia, the devil was actually able to gain control, not merely over individuals but over a whole church. Paul wrote, "O foolish Galatians! Who has bewitched you, before whose eyes Jesus Christ was publicly portrayed as crucified?" (Gal. 3:1-2).

Other New Testament writings also reveal some of the early Christians succumbed to deceitful spirits and the doctrines of demons (1 Tim. 4:1).

In every case I have known of genuine possession problems in believers there has always been a definite traceable reason why they have become so very troubled. Sometimes they have actually had fellowship with demons by engaging in the occult, either before or after conversion (1 Cor. 10:20-21). Other ways I have known Satan to gain a hold on believers are:

1. Inadequate renunciation of sin.
2. Prolonged sinful disobedience to Christ.
3. Engagement in sexual perversions and pornography.
4. The continual use of hard drugs.
5. Rebellion against Jesus.
6. Failure to yield every area of life to Christ. (This leaves Satan in control of some territory in the soul.)
7. Straying back into the world.
8. Constant indulgences in temper or violence.

In most cases of such failures in the Christian life, deep repentance, renunciation, confession and faith in God's forgiving love are sufficient to restore the penitent. However, sometimes where Satan has definitely used the Christian's weakness to reestablish his rule, deliverance ministry has been necessary. Only then has the Christian been restored to fellowship and begun to enjoy again the victorious life of the people of God.

This victorious life, triumphing in the face of overwhelming spiritual odds, is possible only for the new generation people. They alone can stand against the onslaught of the devil. They know that they can win though because of the victory of their Savior Jesus, the supernatural superpower. He has defeated all the forces of wickedness and now has a status high above all principalities and powers and every name that can be named, not only in this world but also in the next (Eph. 1:15-23).

True believers cannot afford to become too preoccupied with Satan's power because they know its boundaries and its limits. They are a people who continually fix their minds on the Lord Jesus Christ. They know that the God of all power and might, the author and giver of all good things, and to whom they belong, will defend them from all evil that may assail body, mind or spirit. The Lord's Prayer, "Lead us not into temptation but deliver us from evil" (Matt. 6:13), is continually answered by God who is their refuge and strength. They are well aware that Satan can ravage the world of men which has given itself to him. They also know that everything the devil does to tempt, assail, harm or overwhelm faithful Christians will be completely reversed for their good.

Satan, in the end, can only further God's purposes for his people. Satan is a defeated foe. Jesus has triumphed (Phil. 2:9-11). This is the news the new generation people should proclaim to the ends of the earth until Jesus returns to establish His glorious kingdom.

11
Exposing the Enemy

Satan, the evil supernatural superpower, though defeated, still is the most subtle of enemies. He is an able master of camouflage, cleverly concealing himself from human sight. He also is brilliant at putting on a vast array of disguises, deceiving men to the point of thinking he doesn't even exist. He has managed to persuade theologians and churchmen that he is simply a figment of the imagination or a mythological character of bygone days. The devil's hiding of himself in this way is a masterpiece of strategy for, in any battle, the enemy must be exposed before he can effectively be opposed.

This revealing of the devil in all his hideous manifestation and evil purposes is the task of the new generation people. They must expose him before the eyes of men as the wicked, perverse superpower that he really is. God has equipped His people for this work by giving them the spiritual gift of discernment (1 Cor. 12:10). This is the specially inspired ability to penetrate through Satan's subtleties, camouflages and disguises to see precisely where he is raising his ugly head. Then they can apply their God-given remedies at the very point of need.

The task of exposing the enemy has to be undertaken on two levels: the first involves a world-scale vision and the second an insight into the personal needs of specific individuals. On the scale of world affairs, the prophets of today, like Amos, Isaiah and Jeremiah of the eighth century B.C., must carefully scrutinize the affairs of men and nations in order to perceive the spiritual forces at work behind them. They must consider daily news reports from a biblical viewpoint, reading between the lines to determine what the devil is scheming in order to bring disruption, disaster and ruin to today's world. It is even more important that they take note of the activities of God in human affairs, knowing that He is weaving together the threads of events in history to achieve his own good purposes for mankind (1 Thess. 4:13).

It is from this standpoint that the new generation people are watchmen sounding the alarms, urging men and nations to repent, believe, and turn to God. How these prophetic voices need to be heard today (1 Thess. 5). God's people must use every means at their disposal, including the news media, and all methods of communication, to get their message across.

The Spirit-filled Christians see not only the pressures deriving from human and economic sources but also the subtle strategies of Satan as they observe occult explosions across the world, the vast march of atheistic, international Communism as they consider the terrifying inflationary climate of the industrial West. As they see the return of the

Jews to Israel, hear of the increasing numbers of earthquakes, together with other signs of the times, God's people know that the return of the Lord Jesus Christ draws near. They have a message that the world needs to hear. They must be faithful to proclaim it (Matt. 24-25).

The insight needed in surveying the vast scale of the global map is also important in dealing with the specific needs of individuals. Every doctor knows that when treating a patient the first essential is to correctly diagnose the root of the trouble. Only then can effective treatment be administered. What applies to the treatment of physical or mental disorders is even more important in ministering to those with afflictions of satanic origin. God-given discernment is essential.

The Lord Jesus Christ, during His earthly ministry, demonstrated the power of discernment in a manner unknown before in human experience. Everywhere He went Satan stood exposed. Demonic forces could not find a hiding place wherever Jesus was present. Jesus always recognized their presence and effectually dealt with them whether they tried to disguise themselves as physical illnesses, emotional disturbances or even as such disciples as Judas and Peter (John 13:1-3; 11, Luke 22:31).

After His ascension, Jesus bestowed this gift of discernment upon the new generation people. In the Acts of the Apostles we see how the enemy stood revealed wherever these dynamic men began to minister. Occult powers could not deceive them even by dressing up as pseudo-spiritual powers. The evil entities always yielded to the superior power of the Spirit of Jesus which inspired His triumphant followers (Acts 5:1-16; 8:7; 13:4-12; 16:17 and others).

This same ability to expose the enemy is just as necessary

for the church today. We are living in a time of rampant occultism and demonic activity unparalleled since the days of the New Testament. It also is evident that to counteract this satanic invasion the Holy Spirit is lavishly endowing his people with supernatural discernment and spiritual power.

I am thankful that when God called my wife and me to a ministry of deliverance He generously equipped us for the task. Time after time devilish forces have been openly exposed at our meetings. Believers have seen displays of demonic activity and Christ's superior power as never before in their lives at our Power, Praise and Healing Services (Luke 4:18-19; 9:1-2, Matt. 10:1).

The gift of discernment has not only been needed to expose genuine demon possession but also to help those who have been suffering from pseudo-possession. Many people who have come to us thinking they were possessed were found to be mistaken. Some of those who cried out seemingly spontaneously at meetings have at times been suffering more from neurosis than possession. Occasionally, very insecure people who have seen films like *The Exorcist* or read about the symptoms of demon possession subconsciously want to use the deliverance ministry as a means of securing the attention they desperately need from sympathetic Christians. These unfortunate people can unwittingly become *spiritual vampires*, drawing energy, power and life from Christians who are abortively trying to exorcise them. Obviously such ministry does not help such people. The ultimate source of their trouble lies elsewhere. They must be pointed lovingly to their real need in order to be genuinely healed.

Discernment is especially needed in cases of mental illness. Those of us who believe in the reality of evil spirits must recognize that a person's mind can become sick as well as his soul or spirit. To treat all fears, depressions or abnormal mental conditions as possession by evil spirits is devastatingly wrong. In fact, it can cause terrible damage to sensitive people. In my ministry I have met several people whose minds have been badly shaken by such treatment at the hands of "would-be" exorcists. It has taken some time to restore them to an even keel, both emotionally and spiritually. One such person was Mavis.

This young lady was a chronic depressive with a tragic history of rejection, failure and hurt. Her hopes of a fulfilling life had been constantly dashed and she suffered also from several physical incapacities which deeply affected her life. She was a very sensitive person, deeply committed as a Christian but quite terrified of disobeying or failing God. She also was extremely confused about such trivial matters as to whether it was sinful for a Christian to wear attractive clothes. She had suffered some sexual abuse and this plagued her conscience.

Church people had tried to help Mavis, treating her as a case for deliverance ministry. At one time she was subjected to two and a half hours of unremitting exorcism during which she became hysterical, violent and abusive. These reactions had been treated as additional demons to be cast out. Battered and bewildered, she turned to me where she felt discernment would be forthcoming. I ministered healing of the memories, a treatment of long duration and taking several sessions in which sins, traumatic experiences and fears are laid open to the healing balm of the Holy Spirit. She is completely healed today.

In our ministry to people with psychological problems we must remember that Jesus came to heal the brokenhearted, the neurotics of today and to set at liberty those who are bruised and demon possessed. We must learn to discern the difference between these sicknesses and minister accordingly.

I have found the same need for care when dealing with physical sicknesses and infirmities which can be caused by germs, accidents, malformations or other material factors. Jesus commissioned His disciples to heal the sick as well as to cast out demons, two quite distinguishable ministries. We need discernment to know the area in which we are operating, otherwise we shall minister with little or no effect. It is obviously ridiculous to treat illnesses which have diagnosable medical causes as if they sprang from the action of evil spirits.

In this respect I well remember the case of Tony, a man in a wheelchair who came to Hainault seeking healing for a condition which kept him completely incapacitated. I was warned by Christians that demons were the cause of his sickness and that he always reacted violently to a healing ministry. As I approached him he roared uncontrollably, went blue in the face, fell out of his wheelchair and began to lash out with his fists.

I quickly enquired of his relatives just how this illness began. They explained that his incapacity was the result of an accident which had caused brain damage and epilepsy. His violence had only been in evidence since he had been told he was possessed. I didn't discern any demonic infiltration into his life and ministered peace and healing to him. When he returned to his senses I explained to him that he had no demons. He was immediately relieved and became as gentle as a lamb. He now is both happy and improved—a really joyous Christian.

"Let those who discerned your demons pray to cast them out," I joked. No one has accepted the challenge because there were never any demons there.

On the other hand, I have known several cases of deliverance which have resulted in the healing of mysterious physical sicknesses. Jesus always was certain of the area with which he was dealing. We must seek the gifts He gives through the Holy Spirit to guide us to a really effective ministry.

A third area where I have needed real discernment has been when confronted by so-called psychosomatic disorders. These are physical symptoms produced by emotional factors. An example is hysterical paralysis which may render a person immobile for long periods without any evident physical reason for the immobility. The distinction between these illnesses and those physical infirmities caused by evil spirits is a very fine one, yet it quite definitely has to be made.

In one rather amusing case of healing, a lady proudly told me that the specialist at the hospital had suggested she see me. She had been complaining of intense pain in her back.

"What did he say caused the pain?" I enquired.

"It is a disease of the spine called psychosomatic," she replied, then added, "but I think it is an evil spirit."

I ministered for wholeness, not exorcism. She had no more trouble and both the specialist and I were well pleased with our powers of discernment.

How can we proceed to a certain diagnosis determining that a sickness has a demonic origin? Foremost, some enquiry into the background of the affliction is necessary, even in cases of extreme emergency. I have learned through much experience how to ask relevant questions quickly. I enquire about the onset of the trouble from the persons themselves if possible and, if not, then from friends and relatives. If the patient has been through a traumatic experience, I minister to the mind. Should definite emotional problems be related to the physical symptoms, I know I am in the realm of the psychosomatic which requires ministry to the whole body, mind and spirit. The most relevant question of all is whether the person has been involved in occult activity, either directly or indirectly. In nearly every case of demon possession I have ever known, the onset of the symptoms coincided with involvement in the occult.

A classic case which illustrates this point occurred recently. A man who implored my help was in very desperate need. His behavior had become uncontrollable. He felt urged to shout out blasphemy in Christian meetings, was hearing voices, and seeing frightening visions. I enquired and discovered that the trouble began with his trying to become a medium twenty years previously. I felt he was possessed. His deliverance was quite remarkable. I found strong resistance to the power of Jesus on the part of the demons who would not obey my command to manifest themselves.

"Could I be wrong in my discernment?" I asked myself. I sought the cooperation of the possessed man by urging him to say, "The blood of Jesus cleanses me from all sin." At this there was an intense reaction by the demons with cries of, "No! No! We possess him."

Three spirits left him. In the end he could shout the words about the blood of Jesus in triumph. He knew he was a free man.

This man had been receiving psychiatric and other medical help for many years. However, it was my privilege through the power of discernment to expose his real enemy and effectively deal with it. Exorcism ministry proved effective where all else had failed.

It is obvious from both the New Testament and from present-day experiences that in the deliverance ministry we may well be dealing with physical and emotional symptoms as well as spiritual sicknesses. Some of the sufferers, like the case above, still may be receiving medical attention when they present themselves for the ministry of exorcism or divine healing. Questions about their medical history sometimes have to be asked. It is helpful that the Anglican "Archbishop's Guide Lines" on exorcism stresses the need for cooperation with the medical profession.

Exorcism is a spiritual ministry for a spiritual sickness, dealing with spiritual symptoms and offering a spiritual remedy but cooperation between doctor, psychiatrist and minister are invaluable for the healing of the whole person. In this way all the resources God has given for the alleviation of suffering are harnessed together for a person's good.

Doctor and psychiatrists may well expose the enemy which, among other things, may be bacteria, brain damage, glandular disorder or emotional stress. It is the task of the new generation people to expose the work of the devil. They can then apply their God-given remedies to bring true spiritual relief and healing to oppressed and suffering souls.

12
The Victorious Legions

During my five years of ministry at St. Paul's Church, Hainault, Essex, which began in September 1970, I was privileged not only to see the formation of a "Divine Turtle" but also to lead a whole army of new generation people in a tremendous onslaught on the kingdom of darkness. This Anglican community became involved in intense spiritual warfare under the banner of the Lord Jesus Christ, the supreme and victorious supernatural superpower.

Week by week, service after service, Satan's captives were delivered from the power of evil spirits as I preached the reality of the victory of Jesus and ministered to them in His wonderful name. It was not just a matter of a powerful individual dispatching Satan's minions to their appointed place, watched by hundreds of cheering spectators. It was a demonstration of the authority of the Body of Christ, the victorious legions of the Lord, engaged in triumphant conflict. Christ's faithful soldiers and servants at St. Paul's were earnest in prayer, praise and faith as together we put the devil's host to flight. The crowds so packed our church that many had to sit in window sills, or stand for hours on the porch, on the church steps, or any other unoccupied space. They were not there simply out of curiosity but rather out of deep need or to be supportive of the healing and deliverance ministry.

All this burst upon me with incredible suddeness and surprise. It was in such marked contrast to my previous years as a Church of England vicar that, at first, I wondered what had happened to me. I was very familiar with administering Holy Communion and conducting evensong, funerals and weddings. I also was expert in arranging social occasions, keeping an eye on the scouts and administering the normal program of an Anglican Church.

This new dimension of ministry certainly took some getting used to. Eventually I realized that I was not participating in anything strange, peculiar or "offbeat." I was taking part in a basic and abiding evangelistic activity of the new generation people of God. As I studied the Bible with my new Holy-Spirit-given insight, I realized that not only had Jesus Christ cast out evil spirits but He had commissioned His disciples to do the same works (Mark 6:13). He had specifically sent them out to preach the Gospel, heal the sick and cast out demons (Mark 3:14-15, Matt. 10:1, Luke 9:1-2). Eventually they returned with joy, saying, "Lord, even the demons are subject to us in your name!" (Luke 10:17).

The Acts of the Apostles relate many incidents of public exorcisms performed by the early Christians after Jesus had risen and ascended to heaven. It is recorded, for instance, that when Philip was ministering in Samaria the crowds paid attention to what he was preaching "when they heard him and saw the signs which he did" (Acts 8:6).

"For unclean spirits came out of many who were possessed, crying with a loud voice, and many who were paralyzed or lame were healed. So there was much joy in that city" (Acts 8:7-8).

I had once thought that the first disciples were unique in Christianity, that what Jesus gave them to do would not necessarily be repeated. I thought that they belonged to a dispensation that had passed away forever. How shortsighted I had been! Now I saw that Jesus' choice of the twelve patriarchs of ancient Israel, the old people of God, so He had chosen twelve disciples to be patriarchs of the church, the new generation people (Mark 3:14-19). The twelve were to be the embryo, the foundation, the nucleus of the true church. It followed, therefore, that all the teaching they received was applicable to the church today. All the promises made to them were for the people of God for all time. So, too, I saw that the commission to spiritual warfare which they had received was to be obeyed by God's people until the Lord returned in glory. The New Testament was not a "once upon a time" story but carried a thrilling living message for our modern world.

Jesus gave the new generation people the most incredible marching orders in history (Matt. 28:18-20, Mark 16:14-17, John 20:21). He gave them power and authority over unclean spirits to cast them out, and to heal every disease and every infirmity and sent them to preach the kingdom of God (Matt. 10:1, Luke 9:1-2, Mark 3:14-19).

They were to set people free and announce the inauguration of Jesus' eternal reign. The Lord promised that the gates of hell should not prevail against them (Matt. 16:18).

They were seemingly just a group of ordinary people with all the weaknesses and failures of the rest of humanity. Peter, their early leader, had once failed Jesus and shown that he could not cope with crisis situations. Can we imagine them—housewives, fishermen, tax-collectors, prostitutes, the uneducated, poor and underprivileged folk—marching out against the legions of hell? By human standards they had little ability and prestige. Jesus had chosen the weak things of the world to confound the mighty (Matt. 5:1-16, 1 Cor. 1:26).

These early Christians appeared to be very ordinary men and women but a supernatural power filled and energized their lives. It came from the same Holy Spirit that had rested upon Jesus; divine, supernatural ability (Acts 1:5-8). Jesus had promised this endowment for his followers after He had defeated Satan in His cosmic victory on the hill of Calvary. He had even asserted that those who believe on Him would not only accomplish the same feats they had seen Him perform but they actually would do even greater works than these (John 14:12).

They had vividly experienced the fulfillment of the Lord's promise at the Festival of Pentecost in the year A.D. 27 (Acts 2:1-4). The wind and fire of the Holy Spirit had filled the Upper Room where they had been praying and they immediately found that they could praise God in languages previously beyond their understanding. Something supernatural had transformed them. Soon they were out in the streets, obeying their God-given orders to the very letter and seeing all Christ's predictions come to pass. The enemy was being routed. The reality of the kingdom of God was being gloriously manifested.

How sad that the church later confused the prestige of wealth, politics, intellect, and worldly securities with the supernatural endowment of the Spirit of God. This vital vision almost petered out. The church today is so often guilty of the same mistakes. The new generation people of God, however, have always been around and we now are living in the time of the greatest revival of spiritual power since the early church. It is happening all over the world. Millions of ordinary men and women are coming alive in the power of the Spirit of God. They are announcing the kingship of Jesus to all who will hear and partake of His blessings.

Exorcism or deliverance ministry, as I prefer to call it, is not a superstitious phenomenon of the Middle Ages. It is a vital demonstration of the power of God through the church's ministry in the scientific and technological age in which we live. It is not an eccentricity of cranky clergy but is faithful to the very spirit and commands of the Lord Jesus. It is an essential factor in the evangelistic ministry of the church, a crucial element in its mission to rescue the lost. Although we must always be watching out for Satan's inroads into the life of the people of God, and may sometimes have to minister deliverance to beleaguered Christians, it still is in our invasion of Satan's territory that we shall meet those who are under subjection to him and need exorcism. The new generation people are an invading force of victorious legions—the only men and women in the world with the supernatural power to deal effectively with the enemy of mankind.

The Holy Spirit has charged the legions of God's people with dynamic supernatural power. It is a spiritual force, a divine energy, which permeates their souls and flows from their prayers, their mouths, their hands, their very beings. This is the basic connotation of the Greek word *dunamis* (power) in the New Testament. It is the word used, for instance, when Jesus said to his disciples, "You shall receive *power* when the Holy Spirit has come upon you" (Acts 1:8).

It is important to realize that Jesus not only bestowed a supernatural energy-type power upon the new generation people but He also gave them that power which derives from authority which in Greek is *exousia*. This is the power which a king, a president or a prime minister exercises by virtue of the status of his office. When Jesus said, "All power *(exousia)* is given unto me in heaven and in earth" (Matt. 28:18). He meant that He now occupied the position of supreme authority in the universe (1 Pet. 3:22, Col. 1:16-23, Phil. 2:9-11). Jesus has the ability to give energy-power and to delegate authority-power to His people.

The manner in which Jesus has bestowed His superlative, supernatural authority upon His people is simple to understand and profound in its effects. He has given them the right to use His name. This confident, believing usage of the name of Jesus of Nazareth will guarantee the availability of all the resources of heaven to the church (John 14:13). We can illustrate this remarkable spiritual truth from parallels in the Middle Ages, modern life, and contemporary legal practice.

One can imagine, for instance, a certain Sir Giles Rochester approaching a Baron's castle in the middle of the night. "Open up!" he cries, standing at the raised drawbridge. "I demand to be given entrance."

The sentries, however, take little notice of him and are all ready to pour a few buckets of boiling water upon this persistent nuisance. The baron certainly will not get out of bed for little Sir Giles. Suddenly, however, the knight changes his tune.

"Open up in the name of the King!" he yells. "I come in the King's name!" How quickly the baron will rouse now, not only to open his gates but to spread out the red carpet. Little Sir Giles has suddenly assumed a new importance and has to be obeyed because he has been vested with the authority of the king. It is as if the king himself stood there. So it is with Christians. Jesus has vested them with His royal splendor and they have the right to use His name.

In modern life a British policeman is a very ordinary man when only wearing his pajamas but when he puts on his uniform he is completely transformed. All traffic comes to a halt at the raising of his hand. Why? The drivers recognize the uniform. This ordinary man now has authority. Behind him are the justices, magistrates, prisons, Parliament and even the Queen. We do as we are commanded. Likewise the name of Jesus is a uniform for Christians. When we wear it, we have an authority derived from heaven itself.

In legal practice, lawyers are familiar with the "power of attorney." This is simply the authority to act in someone's name in his or her absence. Through this legal technique one can control the administration of another's affairs. The power, once given, is complete and absolute. Jesus, likewise, has given His people the power of attorney to look after His affairs until He returns in glory.

Once we have truly understood the nature of our authority and really begin to use it, Satan and his legions tremble (Phil 2:9-11). We, the victorious legions of God, can come against all the powers of darkness in the name of the King of kings. His name is the uniform we wear. He has given us the power of attorney. All we do in His name bears the stamp of His authority (Acts 3:16; 4:30; 16:18).

I learned this lesson from the Bible and from my own experience of spiritual warfare. In one of my first encounters with an evil spirit the demon in the woman asked, "Who are you? Who do you think you are?"

Taken completely by surprise, I replied, "I'm Trevor Dearing."

"I'm not afraid of you. You have no power over me," came the retort. Suddenly I realized the demon was challenging my authority.

"But I come in the name of Jesus. I come against you in the name of the King of kings," I shouted confidently.

"Have mercy! Have mercy! I'm afraid of Jesus," the demon squeaked.

From the moment that I used the name of Jesus, the name of the King, the issue never was in doubt. The woman was set free. I had used the power of attorney given to me by Jesus. All His power was behind me. It was as if Jesus stood there in the flesh, confronting this demonic power. The result was inevitable.

We can even take command over voodooism in the name of Jesus as I did in the case of Maureena. What an experience! Maureena, a heavily built, West Indian woman stood rooted to the spot, dazed with shock and terror. She had just discovered an emblem of a black cockerel on a red triangular piece of cotton material. It had been significantly placed on the white sill of the kitchen window in her London home.

The terror of that chilling curse made her tremble with fear. She stared, utterly petrified, and fully certain she soon would be dead. She had to escape the spell. But how?

She raced from her home as one demented, seeking refuge among friends. For two years she had been tormented in horrible, indescribable ways, quite unable to cope with her job as a teacher of handicapped children and to care for herself and small daughter.

Finally the voodoo terrors began to grip her even tighter with no escape from the chilling curse and the frightening hallucinations became worse. Compulsions and fear often drove her to violence. Once she tried to kill her daughter while the child was asleep. She knew enough about God to pray the "Our Father" and "I believe," thus the tragedy was averted. On another occasion she tried to throttle two Pentecostal pastors who were trying to exorcise her. They were only saved when one of them struggled free from her grip, grabbed a phone and dialed 999 for help. The bobbies took the struggling Maureena off to a mental hospital and during that first night the powerful woman was often uncontrollable.

I first met Maureena at St. Paul's when she came alone for help. Five minutes after the service started, Maureena suddenly pitched senseless to the floor. I immediately sensed a voodoo curse and knew that there would have to be a fantastic scrap before she could be free. Voodoo is a system of magic worship practiced by West Indies Negroes and Creoles, and once a curse is put on someone it can mean the end of their sanity and even the individual's life.

This voodoo spell nearly spelled the end of my life. As I began to pray for Maureena, she spat at me, growled like an animal, bared her teeth and sprang toward me like a rabid jungle beast. Her hands reached for my throat in an attempt to tear me apart. Stewards came dashing forward and did what they could to restrain her, but it was the power of Jesus that held those hideous demonic forces at bay as I began to cast out the voodoo spirit. For ten horrifying minutes the battle raged and eventually, as the sweat poured down her ebony face, the evil spirit left her and she was free. Glory be to Jesus!

The change that came over Maureena was almost unbelievable. She began to smile, beaming a real love for Jesus towards me and the praising congregation. She had been transformed by Jesus, the great deliverer, but strangely she remembered nothing of the deadly struggle that released her.

113

Maureena, now in her right mind, is back teaching handicapped children—a committed Christian and powerful witness for Jesus Christ.

It is a breath-taking thought that Christians actually share the status of their Lord when dealing with the evil supernatural superpower. Through this they have authority over all the powers of the enemy (Eph. 1:15-23). The name of Jesus, however, is not simply a magical potent. It has to be used with confidence and conviction, springing from a certainty of His supreme lordship. Only then will we know the victory (Mark 16:17). This truth is illustrated in the biblical incident concerning the seven sons of Sceva, itinerant Jewish exorcists (Acts 19:13-20). They had seen Paul's power over evil spirits and recognized that it greatly exceeded their own. They had heard him use the name of Jesus and thought they would try the same technique. The evil spirit told them, "Jesus I know and Paul I know, but who are you?"

The man in whom the evil spirit resided leaped on them and overcame them and prevailed against them, so they fled out of the house naked and wounded.

They became the first recorded "streakers" in history.

Demons will always acknowledge the ministry of true believers who, without fear and knowing that the issue is not in doubt, minister in the power and authority derived from their Lord's victory upon the cross.

Some contemporary *would-be* exorcists, although definitely Christians, fail in their ministry not because they lack knowledge of Jesus but because they treat exorcism as some impersonal form, rite or ceremony. They resort to churchianity rather than to the methods of New Testament Christianity. It is important to see that in the ministry of Jesus and the early Christians no particular place, practice, form of prayer, dress, or visual aid was needed. The ministry was powerful, extempore, personal, spontaneous, public, on the spot and complete.

Exorcism is a conflict between persons, not forces. Jesus, the minister, the possessed, and the demon are all involved. During the ministry demons sometimes use the vocal chords of the afflicted sufferer to name themselves, argue, and even refuse to go. The exorcist, as a believing person, will be dealing with the personality of the evil spirit through the personality of the possessed soul. The victory is won always in the name of Jesus which is not simply a form of words, but expresses the supremacy of the person of the exalted Lord.

Because the demonic force is personal, it is important to bind it and render it helpless to harm anyone. To do this we use the power of binding given to the church by the Lord. I have heard all sorts of stories about demons passing from one person into another and even from humans into animals. Such ideas are not without scriptural foundation because we do read in the Scriptures of an incident where Jesus allowed a whole army of demons to go from a man into a herd of swine (Mark 5:1-20). The swine rushed down a steep hill and into the sea.

I was present once when a demon passed out of a person into a dog and the dog rolled over on its back in a frenzy. It too had to be exorcised and once that was done the animal settled down to sleep, none the worse for its experience. Once I learned the power of binding, the problem no longer existed. No one in my experience has ever suffered as the result of someone else's deliverance from evil spirits.

Where do these bound spirits go when once cast out? One thing is certain. We cannot pass final judgment upon these fallen spirits no more than we can upon fallen human beings. We cannot send them to hell. Judgment belongs only to the

Lord who has prepared a lake of fire for the devil and all his angels (Matt. 25:41). A passage in the New Testament speaks of spirits in prison (1 Pet. 3:19). It seems there is a spiritual underworld, netherland or pit, where bound spirits await the judgment of Christ (2 Pet. 2:4).

Once again it must be emphasized that this apparently incredible ministry is not the warfare of solitary crusaders but of the whole army of God's new generation people. It is for this reason that I always have felt it right to minister deliverance in the presence and with the support of the whole company of believers. These gatherings have never been simply for the curious sensation-seekers but rather occasions for demonstrating the reality of the church's ministry of deliverance. Through this glorious ministry hundreds of people in my experience have seen the reality of the lordship of Jesus and placed their trust in Him.

It is remarkable that such seemingly weak, ordinary people as ourselves have been entrusted with such power and authority. What weapons of warfare our Jesus has given to us! Through them we are able to deliver our fellowmen from those forces of evil which emanate from the devil. We certainly are the victorious legions of God as we fulfill His command to "Preach the Gospel, heal the sick and cast out demons." We reecho the cry of the first disciples, "Lord, even the demons are subject to us in your Name (Luke 10:17).

"Rejoice," He replies, "even more that your names are written in heaven" (my paraphrase, Luke 10:20).

13
Caring for the Casualties

Many of the people who came to St. Paul's were in desperate need. Over the years the numbers who sought our help multiplied so rapidly that one of our church members observed wryly, "This place shouldn't be called St. Paul's Church any longer. It should be St. Paul's Hospital."

In a way he was right. In any warfare there are bound to be casualties who need sympathy, love, and help in very practical ways. So as the new generation people advance into enemy-occupied territory of human souls, they need a spiritual Red Cross service with them to care for the men and women who have suffered the ravages of the enemy.

This became obvious to me from the very start. Olive, my first case of deliverance, needed nearly three years of love, counsel and advice before she was able to stand on her own feet as a Christian. Only then could she resist the attempts of the enemy to assail her. Those who give the impression that we can minister deliverance to people and then simply walk away are failing in their understanding of Christian responsibility. Aftercare is essential for those who have been deeply wounded by the devil. Deliverance ministry must always be closely associated with pastoral care. Consequently, I have always been very careful to ensure the availability of such help for all to whom I minister.

The most serious danger facing those who have been exorcised is that of reentry. Jesus taught the reality of this possibility.

"When the unclean spirit has gone out of a man, he passes through waterless places seeking rest; and finding none he says, 'I will return to my house from which I came.' And when he comes he finds it swept and put in order. Then he goes and brings seven other spirits more evil than himself, and they enter in and dwell there; and the last state of that man becomes worse than the first" (Luke 11:24-26).

I have seen several cases of reentry. One was Barbara. She was completely delivered at one of our Tuesday evening meetings. In the ensuing days she was radiant, declaring to one and all the reality of her release from the powers that had possessed her. She was peaceful, happy, relaxed and free. The voices that had tormented her had ceased. She could pray with reality and read her Bible with understanding.

Later, against my advice and before she was remotely ready to do so, she insisted on going back to the place where she had engaged in prostitution. Within a short time she returned to St. Paul's seeking urgent help and in a terrible state of repossession. Her condition, in fact, was worse than when we first ministered to her.

Experiences of this sort have taught me the essentials of

the aftercare needed by those who have been severely oppressed or possessed by the powers of darkness. Immediate counseling is imperative to make certain that the patient has been completely released and is at peace. We also have to ascertain that there has been real repentance for every sin the enemy used to ensnare the afflicted person and that there has been a definite renunciation of the world, the flesh and the devil.

Enquiry must be made into the circumstances which led the person into satanic bondage in order to ensure a complete break with past occult involvement. Sometimes this involves the severing of all relationships with occultists, the ending of immoral associations, and even the burning of books, charms or other objects connected with occult practices. A change of address or employment may be necessary also. Occasionally we have had to make arrangements to visit the person's home and exorcise the rooms, symbolically sealing the windows and doors in the precious name of Jesus.

I have also celebrated the Holy Communion in such homes and blessed the house in the name of the Father, Son and Holy Spirit. I have claimed all the promises of Psalm 91 for the inhabitants of the house. "No evil shall befall you, no scourge come near your [home]. For he will give his angels charge of you to guard you in all your ways" (vv. 10,11).

In dealing with the past we also may have to exercise the ministry of the healing of the memories—memories perhaps of Satan's tormenting of the soul, or of other sinister happenings which need to be brought to the healing light of Christ. In one instance I had to ask the Lord to heal a man's memory of occult experiences as a child. The sufferer's parents had been mediums, holding seances in their home. They had insisted on their little son attending them and he

119

carried in manhood terrible memories of a darkened room, an organ playing, and a croaking voice talking about the "departed." These experiences were used by the devil to haunt him.

Satan, I discovered, has come down memory lane often to harass those who were once his captives. In order to counteract this insidious tactic I have prayed to God and commanded the devil along the following lines: "Father, in the name of Jesus, and in the power of the Holy Spirit, I close the door of this heart against any reentry by Satan. Amen. Devil, I rebuke you! You shall not come down the avenue of the past to hurt this child of God! I break all past connections you have had with this soul. You shall not play on his memories to hurt or assail him! Go, forever, in the name of Jesus."

Often it has taken some time before the wounds finally have been healed and the released person has been able to turn his eyes from the troubles of the past and to the present reality of Jesus who gives new hope and confidence for the future.

In order for rehabilitation to be complete there are other problems often in the released person's life which have to be dealt with. Satan will have sought to destroy not only his victim's mind, but also the very circumstances of his experience. Marital problems are common causes of concern in this respect. Marriage as the deepest and most intimate of human relationships will almost certainly have been terribly disrupted by the sufferer's spiritual condition. The deliverance ministry, with proper aftercare, has frequently resulted in new Christian homes of love and peace.

Other environmental problems which can retard progress involve relationships with parents, relatives and friends. All anxieties and stresses involving anything from money to sex, failures and purposelessness, have to be faced and resolved. This may, on occasions, involve cooperation with doctors, psychiatrists, social workers, and even employers. Those who sincerely seek to help the oppressed and possessed must be prepared to undertake much more than a few minutes of encouraging conversation. They are involved in the healing of the whole person in the whole of life.

For this reason, as with the ministry of deliverance, the aftercare of spiritual casualties should be the concern not only of individuals but of the entire church. People who have been in the power of the enemy need the whole body of believers to shield, support and pray for them. The important element in the church's ministry to the needy is the actual showing of love. Those who have been in Satan's grip, almost without exception, have suffered terrible rejection at the hands of their fellows.

In my examination of many case histories of demon possession, I have discovered that the most common factor is this terrible rejection by parents, teachers, friends, relatives, society and sadly, even the church. These poor people have become spiritual drop-outs, easy prey for Satan.

Once delivered they frequently are still fearful of being rejected again and sometimes this delays their recovery. They often cling to sympathetic people, making demands upon them which are very exhausting. They are attention seekers par excellence. It is obvious that they need a very accepting relationship on the part of the whole church community in which they have sought help. They need all the love of Jesus that His people can possibly give. This does not mean that they can be indulged in all their demands. Once the accepting relationship has been established, firmness and discipline also are necessary for their healing, especially in setting the bounds of time and energy within which they can be helped. Gently, loving, yet firmly, they must learn to trust their fellow Christians and stand upon their own feet.

We found at St. Paul's Church that the casualties of spiritual warfare were much helped by the quiet atmosphere of small fellowship groups, usually meeting in homes. There they could assimilate Christian truths and love through Bible study and deep personal contact with other Christians in manageable numbers. In this relaxed atmosphere they were able to grow in the knowledge and love of God as they shared their problems, asked questions and received reassurance. There they made Christian friends whom they knew they could trust and call upon in time of need. In these groups delivered people were especially taught the truths about the supremacy of the power of their newly found Lord—supremacy over all the forces which had assailed them.

They were shown how they could put their trust in Christ and stand upon his promises. They began to realize that no counterattacks by the evil supernatural superpower could ever separate them from God's love and care. We had the joy of seeing many such people not only become able to withstand all the assaults of the enemy but also take their place in the victorious legions of God, aggressively invading Satan's domain.

My engagement in spiritual warfare and concern for the aftercare of the casualties inevitably led me to see the need for special centers to care for the most critical cases of souls devastated by satanic activities. Ministers and churches sometimes feel that the needs of these people are beyond their ability to supply in time, energy or experience. Some casualties are too deeply wounded to be cared for in ordinary homes, especially where young children are to be found.

Most families are just not geared to the rehabilitation of very emotionally disturbed people. They need specialists in spiritual care.

Once I had seen the need, I began to act. We made a determined, yet sadly abortive attempt to build such a center on wasteland behind St. Paul's Church. In the end local opposition to the scheme prevailed. How pleased I was then that we were always able to refer serious cases to other local Christian centers where they received considerable help. It is a cause for thanksgiving that as the church's ministry of deliverance becomes more necessary than ever in the days in which we live, such centers, by the providence of God, are springing up all over the world. They have a vital part to play in caring for the casualties of our increasing, but ever victorious conflict with the powers of evil. The devil seems to be making a last desperate attempt to capture the hearts of men before the Lord's return to establish His kingdom on earth. However, we can rejoice that our glorious God is moving by His Spirit, and through His people to reclaim the lost and rescue Satan's captives.

"*Rise up, O men of God!*
Have done with lesser things;
Give heart and soul and mind and strength
To serve the King of kings."
"Rise Up, O Men of God"
William P. Merrill

14
The Supernatural Superpowers

In the year 1976 a candidate for the presidency of the United States of America stated: "I think we still have superiority over Russia in the multiplicity of delivery systems for atomic weapons and our ability to defend ourselves. We are not vulnerable to attack from Russia except through weapon deliveries. We've got too many support troops per combat troop—about twice as many as the Soviet Union. We've got 700 atomic bombs in Korea. . . ."

He was facing the harsh realities of life in the 1970s, and he had not yet spoken about the threat of Communist China. Britain and France, we know, also have nuclear strike forces. All these nations seek to preserve a very delicate balance of power.

Yet we have always dreamed of peace and paradise. Our aspirations and longings have always been in that direction.

Poets have written about it. This vision fills the pages of our best literature and is a constant theme of the songs and lyrics of the centuries. Yet, we have never been able to achieve it. We have made advances in science, technology and education. Economists and politicians have planned a better society and every war has been "the war to end all wars." Tragically, however, the twentieth century has seen the most horrible and bloody encounters in human history. Suffering has been intense. We have continually failed in our most desired objective—peace on earth! Is our struggle then only with ourselves? No! Paul's words tell us:

"For we are not contending against flesh and blood, but against the principalities, against the powers, against the world rulers of this present darkness, against the spiritual hosts of wickedness in the heavenly places" (Eph. 6:12).

This insight is as relevant to the situations reported in the newspapers of today as it was to the thought of the first century A.D.. The devil was vitally active in causing the First World War. Later, he was behind the rise of Hitler and Nazi Germany. Through this dictator, Satan caused a whole nation to believe a lie and a bloody orgy ensued (2 Cor. 4:4).

The devil is at work in the world today in the rise of atheistic Communism and its rapid progress. He is behind the seemingly threatening conflict between Russia and China, and between East and West. He has plotted and brought to pass the decadence of Western society, sowing seeds of corruption through the mass communications media, selfish capitalism and extreme trade unionism. He is behind all racial tension and conflict and rejoices at the troubles in Ireland. This evil supernatural superpower is the force to be reckoned with in today's world, seeking always to frustrate God's purposes for mankind.

Satan has set up a kingdom to rival and imitate that of

God. He has followed the divine blueprint and established a parallel evil force to oppose all that is good. The devil imagines himself to be as God, supreme ruler of the universe with a special interest in planet earth. He has raised up fallen princelings—principalities— to emulate the glorious archangels of heaven. Little demons or unclean spirits compete with God's angels to minister to the hearts of men. He has provided himself a territory, the occult realm, over which he already reigns. He is calling into being the person of an antichrist to establish a fictitious messiahship reign over men on earth.

The spirit of this antichrist is already at work in the world and the occult is the current expression of his deceiving power. He has even offered to men spurious spiritual gifts such as spirit-healing and counterfeit tongues with clairvoyance and soothsaying to parallel the precious Holy Spirit ministries of knowledge and prophecy. Through these counterfeits he has succeeded in leading many thousands of people into terrible bondage and possession because of their curiosity and even their sincere seeking after truth. The new generation people must constantly expose this satanic deception and warn mankind of the dangers of trespassing into this "no-go" area of false spirituality.

Some recent controversies about exorcism have been concerned solely with the deliverance of individuals. This issue involves humanity as a whole. The world needs exorcism; nations needs exorcism! We need to see the handwriting of the devil across the pages of history. He is still making his mark on both national and international affairs today. He is the god of this world. The whole world lays in the hands of the evil one (1 John 5:19).

In my own particular ministry, as in the Bible, I have constantly met the devil on the level of personal lives and problems. Human beings can be harassed, tempted and tormented by the devil and his minions. If they give themselves to him through willful sin or engagement in dangerous, forbidden occult practices, then whole areas of their personality can be brought into bondage to this evil supernatural superpower. Ultimately demons may even possess them, completely rule them, making life intolerable. The evil superpower is behind everything that is alien to the life of man, including psychoses and physical sickness. He uses all sorts of tensions, pressures, germs and other allies to hurt and destroy our lives.

I admit that all this cannot be proved by scientific techniques because this personal evil life-force is not within the normal orbit of the eyes, ears or other senses. By definition he is a supernatural being beyond them. To see this as reality is not a feat of the intellect but by the operation of a sixth sense, a spiritual insight which penetrates beyond appearances to their ultimate causation. It is the eye of the seer and the prophet which apprehends evil and plots its course. It is the work of the Holy Spirit which opens our eyes and inspires our souls.

Once we have caught the vision we must interpret it to our fellows that their eyes too may be opened because finally only those remain blind who do not wish to see. To really face our problems we must see that we are not living merely on one planet in a vast material universe but that we are set in spiritual dimensions of life. We must comprehend the astounding fact that supernatural forces are influencing human life today. That takes care of the bad news. Now, for the good.

If our perception stopped at this point there would be no hope for the human race because the spiritual superpowers bent on our destruction cannot be assailed or destroyed by nuclear or any other weapons. They are evil spirits vastly superior to any man-developed power. So, what is our good news? It is graphically proclaimed for us in the Bible, the inspired Word of God. It also is constantly verified in our day-by-day experiences. The ultimate and supreme spiritual super Power is God—Father, Son and Holy Spirit. The Father created mankind for himself and loves us with an everlasting love. The Son, Jesus, swept through the eternal dimension into the realm of space and time and, at Calvary, triumphed over all the spiritual hosts of wickedness. When He cried, "It is finished!" He scattered them all in disarray. By the power of His resurrection He has called into being a new race, the new generation people who live in the power of the Holy Spirit.

We have been promised that the gates of hell shall not prevail against us. We are enabled to withstand all the devil's assaults as we move together like a massive spiritual turtle. From this standpoint we can see the devil in his right perspective, limited by the sovereign power of God—defeated by Christ—and constantly rendered ineffective by the power of the Holy Spirit. We know that in the end God can turn even the apparent success of the devil to serve his purposes. Christians, therefore, do not dwell obsessively or neurotically upon the superpower of evil. We are not so much devil-conscious as Jesus-conscious. We are Jesus-oriented in every aspect of our lives.

Although we rightly see the ultimate issues as spiritual, yet the new generation people realize that the evil supernatural superpower has to be fought on many fronts. We are not in any competition with men of good will but join forces with all truly sincere human endeavors for the alleviation of suffering and distress. We who are true to our vision will certainly be engaged in spiritual warfare as the victorious legions of God's people. We shall constantly and energetically be about our business of "preaching the Gospel, healing the sick and casting out demons."

We shall be rising up to bind those principalities and powers which are endeavoring to disrupt the life of mankind. If we are true to our vision, we shall be active in and with the medical profession, Christian educators, businessmen, social servants, union leaders, economists, politicians and all that is worthwhile for the well-being of mankind. Every sphere and area of human life must be claimed for Christ and His glorious kingdom. We will bring our God-given insights and freedoms to these pursuits earnestly praying, "Thy will be done on earth, as it is in heaven."

This petition of the Lord's Prayer involves God's people in dealing with practical issues and environmental problems as well as spiritual bondages. We also realize and face up to the evil which is in the human heart in addition to that which stems directly from the alien spiritual superpower. We will seek to apply the divine and ultimate remedy to every need and not simply skate on the surface of human life.

We shall be urgent in prayer, constant in faith and zealous in our actions as we engage in that victorious warfare against all the powers of darkness to which our Lord has commissioned us. We will bind and loose, release, protect, deliver and rehabilitate in obedience to our Lord's command (Matt. 12:29; 16:19). We will be vividly aware that we wage this warfare, not in solitary sentry posts, but as a mighty army marching as to war, realizing that the ministry of the new generation people has never been more relevant than it is today.

We, the supernaturally anointed people of God, though conscious of our inevitable human weaknesses, are fully aware of our spiritual endowment with the power and authority of the Lord Jesus Christ, the victorious supernatural superpower. He promised, "You will receive power when the Holy Spirit has come upon you." We realize therefore that we are the only people in the world who can bring spiritual release and deliverance to a beleaguered human race.

We not only provide a shelter in the midst of our spirit-filled community life, we are commissioned by our Lord to be on the attack and wage warfare in his name. Hallelujah! Already we see the powers of darkness shaken as we perceive the Lord Jesus Christ at the right hand of the majesty on high. We confidently declare the victory of our Lord. We declare the victory not only to the people of this world but to the principalities and powers.

"That through the church the manifold wisdom of God might now be made known to the principalities and powers in the heavenly places" (Eph. 3:10).

"Hallelujah! For the Lord our God, the Almighty, reigns" (Rev. 19:6).